THE
GOLDEN
AGE

ALSO BY EDITH GROSSMAN

The Antipoetry of Nicanor Parra

TRANSLATIONS BY EDITH GROSSMAN

Don Quixote (Miguel de Cervantes)

Memories of My Melancholy Whores (Gabriel García Márquez)

Living to Tell the Tale (GGM)

News of a Kidnapping (GGM)

Strange Pilgrims (GGM)

Of Love and Other Demons (GGM)

The General in His Labyrinth (GGM)

Love in the Time of Cholera (GGM)

Captain of the Sleepers (Mayra Montero)

Deep Purple (MM)

The Red of His Shadow (MM)

The Last Night I Spent with You (MM)

The Messenger (MM)

In the Palm of Darkness (MM)

The Feast of the Goat (Mario Vargas Llosa)

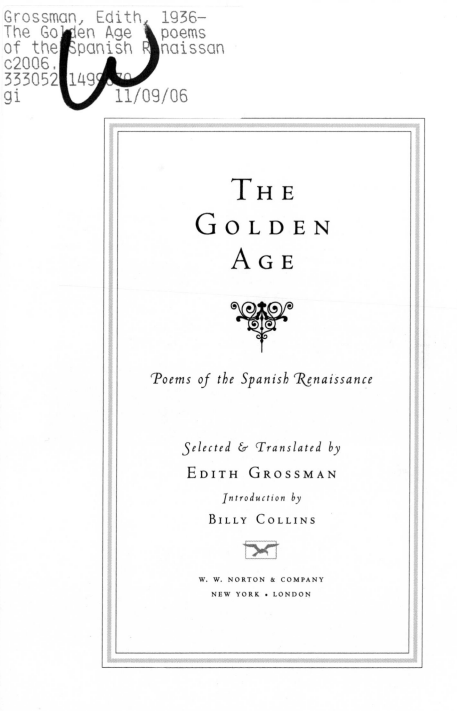

THE
GOLDEN
AGE

Poems of the Spanish Renaissance

Selected & Translated by

EDITH GROSSMAN

Introduction by

BILLY COLLINS

W. W. NORTON & COMPANY
NEW YORK · LONDON

Spanish text of the poems reprinted with the generous permission of Elias L. Rivers
from *Renaissance and Baroque Poetry of Spain.* New York: Dell Publishing Co., 1966.

Manufacturing by Maple-Vail Book Manufacturing Group
Book design by Chris Welch
Production manager: Julia Druskin

Library of Congress Cataloging-in-Publication Data

The Golden Age : poems of the Spanish Renaissance / selected &
translated by Edith Grossman ; introduction by Billy Collins.
p. cm.
ISBN-13: 978-0-393-06038-6 (hardcover)
ISBN-10: 0-393-06038-1 (hardcover)
1. Spanish poetry—Classical period, 1500–1700—Translations into
English. 2. Spanish poetry—Classical period, 1500-1700. I. Grossman,
Edith, 1936–
PQ6267.E3G76 2006
861'.308—dc22
                                    2006018052

W. W. Norton & Company, Inc., 500 Fifth Avenue, New York, N.Y. 10110
www.wwnorton.com

W. W. Norton & Company Ltd., Castle House, 75/76 Wells Street, London W1T 3QT

1 2 3 4 5 6 7 8 9 0

To Elias L. Rivers,
with many thanks.

CONTENTS

List of Illustrations

INTRODUCTION

Billy Collins

Many years ago, a teacher of mine tipped off us students that no matter which historical period we were studying, two statements could always be applied: 1) the middle class was expanding; and 2) it was an age of contradictions. Mercifully, no more history tests lie ahead of me, but this bit of insider advice, especially the second verity, came to mind when I turned my attention to the contents of Edith Grossman's *The Golden Age: Poems of the Spanish Renaissance.*

The drastic contradictions that marked the history of sixteenth- and seventeenth-century Spain involved, on the one hand, the country's growth as a major European and colonial power and, on the other, the spreading virus of religious intolerance, racial purism (*limpieza de sangre*), and xenophobia. The period did see the founding of universities and a rich blossoming in the arts, particularly painting, but when religious and racial persecution became institutionalized as never before in European history, the long shadow of the

Inquisition fell across this era of creative ferment. Jews and Moors who claimed they had converted (*conversos*) were the initial victims of the inquisitors, but as the nets of suspicion were cast more broadly, persecution became rampant. In those days, as would happen centuries later during America's McCarthy years, it was easy for individuals to get into ideological and doctrinal trouble. Even St. Teresa of Ávila was investigated. Religious factions and rival orders of priests fought bitterly over matters of belief and liturgy. It is not surprising, therefore, that four of the six Spanish poets included in this volume were either imprisoned, exiled, or both.

It is curious, however, that one cannot apprehend any of this torment just from reading the dominant poetry of the time, which simply remains silent on the subject. Forbidden to write about tyrannical rulers, the poets of the Golden Age chose to look back to other golden ages for their subjects and style rather than recount the disturbing history that was taking shape before their eyes. The traditional sonnet, the eclogue, and the song were the forms into which these poets poured their sentiments. But if poetry is "the news that stays new," as Ezra Pound would have it, perhaps it must avoid keeping up with the headlines, at the risk of becoming mere news itself—that is, writing that is read only once. The absence of trauma in the poetry of a distant era should not wholly surprise a contemporary audience that has grown accustomed to the lure of subjectivity and personal observation over the noise of "current events." Poetry has an aesthetic mission to follow, which requires allegiance to the decorum of the time, if only to exhaust the possibilities of its conventions so that a poetry of the future can break entirely free of them. A true "cult of originality" would not appear in Spain for another century.

These new translations by Edith Grossman provide us with a well-chosen sampling of the work of the major poets of the Golden

Age. Grossman has decided—wisely, I would say—to leave the poems in the diction of their own time rather than recasting them in contemporary language, thus maintaining their original tone. The resulting volume gives us new access to these often neglected poems, and, incidentally, it gives me a chance to make a few observations about the poets gathered here and their golden output.

In 1526 a meeting took place between the Barcelona poet Juan Boscán and the ambassador from Venice, Andrea Navagero, during which the ambassador convinced Boscán that the way to resuscitate Spanish poetry was through the use of Italian models, particularly the Petrarchan love sonnet. Garcilaso de la Vega, Boscán's friend, was quick to adopt the Petrarchan style, thus perpetuating the language and metaphors of the courtly love traditions of the Troubadours. To this day, no one seems to know whether courtly love, which inspired a literary genre based on the worship of unattainable women, was simply a poetic phenomenon or the actual practice of knights. It could have been the expression of a class anxiety stimulated by the lack of privacy in medieval castle life and, therefore, secretive and illicit. Most likely it was something in between—a kind of flirtatious game, part playful, part serious, and largely intended as a source of upper-class entertainment. Whatever the historic truth, the love poems of Garcilaso and others follow the conventional role-playing of the desperate lover seeking the pity of an unachievable woman whose beauty is surpassed only by her cruel indifference to his entreaties.

Combining Neo-Platonic idealism with a masochistic taste for suffering, courtly love poems thus portray the lover himself as lost at sea, disoriented, shipwrecked, imprisoned and—frighteningly— "chained and shackled in the shell of Venus." At the same time, amorous similes flatter the beloved by comparing her hair to gold, her complexion to lilies and roses, her bosom to snow, her mouth to coral, her eyes to blinding suns. This extension of courtly love rituals centuries beyond their medieval origins might seem to suggest an approaching decadence—that stage where the style outlasts the reality of the content—but as C. S. Lewis points out in *The Allegory of Love*, these new ideas about the service, the code, and the ennobling power of love are present throughout history—from the original poetry of the Troubadours all the way to the amorous poetry and popular songs of the present day.

Jorge Manrique's elegy for his father, the first translation in this volume, is a good example of how the poetry of this period relied on a set of conventional themes. The poem is a showcase of sentiments common to medieval Christian literature. Time is fleeting so we must amend our lives. The world is a pathway to the hereafter. Human wishes arise from vanity and are, indeed, pursued in vain. All that is earthly is mutable. Beauty fades. The mighty are strapped to the turning wheel of Fortune, and as they rise so shall they fall. Thus, the major literary chords of *ubi sunt*, *de casibus*, and *sic transit gloria mundi* are struck resoundingly. But against the background of these standard motifs, moments of Manrique's original thinking shine forth. If we concentrate on the present moment, he claims in his elegy, the future will be made to seem as illusory as the past: "we will deem the yet to come / as past and gone." Manrique's new imagery invigorates the familiar themes. As both small streams and mighty rivers disappear into the ocean, he writes, so individual lives, whether ordinary or exalted, will become equal in death. The wheel of caprice is a conventional trope, but not the connection Manrique makes between the joys of life and "racing horses" carrying us uncontrollably and perilously ahead, or his reduction of the world's most lavish possessions to "fleeting dewdrops in the fields."

Like other poets gathered here, Fray Luis de León was a priest who spent time in prison. An Augustinian, he was attacked as a heretic by rival Dominican professors at the University of Salamanca, who also resented his Jewish origins and his emphasis on the Hebrew roots of the Bible. A kind of Christian Horace, he praised the simple life of the countryside though he hardly experienced plain-living in his time. His "Ode III" combines a tribute to the blind composer Francisco Salinas with a meditation on the progress of the soul from heaven to earth then back to its eternal home. According to his scheme, the soul enters the world from a state of preexistence similar to that of the Wordsworthian baby, who comes into the realm of matter "trailing clouds of glory." The evocative "Ode VIII: Quiet Night" opens with the conventional dichotomy between the wakeful light of heaven and the soporific darkness of the earth; but then the poem develops into a celebration of the astronomical wonders of the heavens, including the moon of wisdom, the "brilliant star of Love," and the symbolic powers of the planets—wrathful Mars, benign Jupiter, and paternal Saturn. The poem closes with a return to earth and the vision of a renewed landscape of fields, meadows, dales, and valleys imbued with truth and delight, sweetness and blessings. By fitting such mystical experiences into five-line stanzas rhyming ababb, the poet demonstrates the critical importance of constrictive form. Any mystical poet must also rely heavily on metaphor, that Aristotelian essential. The solar system, particularly the Pythagorean music of the spheres, is Luis de León's most habitual metaphor, just as St. John of the Cross favors the arms of a lover.

And so we come to the supreme exemplar of Spanish mysticism, "the ecstatic Doctor," who sought to express moments of divine union in the language of human passion. St. Teresa commanded San Juan de la Cruz to write instructive sayings meant to help postulants along the road to the mystical life, and that's how he might have begun his own path. But his poetry, some of it written in jail in Toledo, soon sprouted visionary wings. The paradox at the heart of his writing is his choice of the language of carnal love to convey transcendent spiritual experiences. The subject here is no longer courtly love based on longing, anticipation, and courtesy; rather it is sexual union approximating the union between man and God. As a result, we readers face a difficult task. When St. John writes that he lowers his face, leaning over his "lover," we cannot help but think of a man leaning over the face of a flesh-and-blood woman, but the higher schematic of his poetry asks us to think metaphorically and not be corrupted by the literal pole of the metaphor. If we are unable to see the language of sexual love as purely symbolic, we can only understand such ecstasies as fleshly joys or as pathologies of sexual repression. The reader must choose between the lower road of Freud and the higher road of mystical union. How are we as mortals to judge the claim that this saint is the bride of Christ? And how do we appraise the scene in which the poet falls down with his lover-God among the lilies and feels the perfumed breath of the Divine on his bosom? Poets turn to metaphor when they are confronted with the ineffable, but the comparison here (sex) competes for attention with the putative subject (God). The same problem of representation confronts Dante, who needs words to describe the vision of the Divine in his *Paradiso*. And in *Paradise Lost* Milton must describe a still unfallen world with a fallen language. How to articulate an essentially nonverbal experience involving an erasure of consciousness? Mystical poetry cannot describe mystical experience, but it can translate supraverbal experience into imagistic and metaphoric language; in St. John's poetry, this means translating downward to the passions of the flesh.

With the influential Luis de Góngora and the controversial Francisco de Quevedo, we move into the heavy embellishment and imagistic excesses of the Spanish baroque style. Gongorism continues the thematic conventions of courtly love poetry, but now with such verbal extravagance that some poems seem in danger of collapsing like unsteady Christmas trees under the sheer weight of their own decoration. The superabundance of imagery at the heart of the baroque can be seen not as flattery but as an attempt to smother women in blandishments, to throw a verbal robe over their naked reality. In one particularly overstuffed sonnet of Quevedo's, the woman's eyes are stars at dawn, her lips are sirens somehow dyed red, and her beauty is springtime itself; meanwhile the lover is a martyr, a delirious idolater, a man lost in "burning snow"—an image that recalls the symptoms of chills and fever which accompany the courtly love-flu. Similar to the fate of the euphuistic style in English prose, the Spanish baroque dies of its own overindulgence, the price of placing the cart of style before the horse of content.

Almost too grand a figure to be contained in this collection, Lope de Vega's massive production—a thousand plays and as many poems—would suffice to put him in a literary class of his own. A spiritual cousin to the English metaphysical poets, Lope de Vega wrote both religious and secular poems and integrated the elements of tension, contradiction, and paradox that would be so dear to the heart of T. S. Eliot. The "Sacred Rhyme" included here is a kind of sinner's prayer, employing the imagery of the lost path, a fall into the "devil's pit," a journey through "a fearsome labyrinth in the dark," and the slaying of "the monster of blind deception." The short poem condenses the adventures of a chivalric romance involving the perilous journey of a knight toward an enlightening destination. The sonnet representing "Human Rhymes" is spoken by a frustrated courtly lover whose plight can only be described as a series of insoluble contradictions, including to go and stay at the same time and to be torn between the eternal and the mundane. In

"Folk Song VII," the convention-breaking use of realism undercuts the poem's Petrarchan conceits by the same negative strategy used in Shakespeare's "Sonnet 130" ("My mistress' eyes are nothing like the sun"). Luscinda's eyes are not at all like stars, her lips fall short of being coral, her bosom is hardly snowy, and her hands are not like lilies. Like Shakespeare's beloved, Luscinda is remarkable for her reality, not just rendered so by the exaggerations of poetic conceits. Lope de Vega is also a playful ironist. "Instant Sonnet" is caught up in itself in a spirit of modernist self-reflexivity. Its subject is its own 14-line progress as it goes along, finally concluding with "I've begun tercet two. I do believe/ I'm coming to the end of thirteen verses;/ see if there are fourteen: the sonnet's done." The poem ends by swallowing its own tail.

I am glad that Edith Grossman decided to stretch the geographic boundaries of this book to include Sor Juana Inés de la Cruz. She is, of course, a Mexican poet, but she also is a key figure in the development of baroque amatory poetry in Spanish. A remarkable figure, she stands virtually alone in her advocacy of the educational rights of women in the Hispanic world. Her "Reply to Sor Filotea," written in prose at the suggestion of a bishop with whom she disagreed about a doctrinal matter, is a vigorous justification of her own career of learning and scholarship. Cleverly argued, her letter claims at one point that she is possessed by an overactive brain that thinks even at night and thus requires a nutritious diet of books to keep it fed. While making a connection between cooking and learning (St. Teresa found God moving "among the saucepans"), she advances a broader argument, a passionate defense of the life of the intellect for women and men alike.

Sor Juana Inés de la Cruz's pen, as Alan Trueblood put it, is often "talking about itself as it writes." Her taste for ironic complexity is evident in "Sonnet 145," a meticulously constructed formal poem that dismisses the value of poetry because it is based on "vanity, contrivance, artifice," deceit, and flattery. "Sonnet 147" accuses the rose of being deceitful in its beauty and truthful only in its death. Her moral seems to be that living is presumptuous, but dying is wise. And this sonnet is followed by an ironic poem about those "lucky" enough to die young and leave behind, as they would say, a beautiful corpse.

Appearing last in the collection, Sor Juana may be viewed as outdoing the other Golden Age poets represented here in advancing the style and attitudes of Renaissance poetry beyond the useful but eventually frayed conventions of the time. The freshness of her work is but one reason this volume is a welcome addition to the importation of Spanish poetry into English.

Somers, New York
February 2006

TRANSLATOR'S INTRODUCTION

The concept of a "golden age" has always been, for me, an idea infused with stubborn mystery. What appears so reluctant to take shape is an explanation of why the phenomenon occurs at all. How does it happen that at certain times in the cultural histories of nations—Athens under Pericles, Florence under the Medicis, England under Elizabeth I, or Latin America in the 1960s—a burst of productivity seems to ignite an entire generation of artists? The nature of the society in which a golden age of the arts flourishes is, apparently, irrelevant. Free or repressive, secular or theocratic, contemporary or ancient—regardless of a nation's social organization or direction, or its political system, an extraordinary, inexplicable explosion of creativity takes place during these unique periods, and just as inexplicably it then fades away. The Spanish Renaissance was one of those times.

Called the *Siglo de Oro*, this brilliant period in Spanish history generally embraces the sixteenth and seventeenth centuries, although within this broad designation, temporal, and even geographical demarcations sometimes blur; in this volume, for instance, I've pushed the notion back a few decades to include the fifteenth-century poet Jorge Manrique, whom many people consider the author of one of the greatest poems in Spanish. I've also expanded the geography by several thousand miles of ocean in order to incorporate in this selection the Mexican Sor Juana Inés de la Cruz, a major voice in Spanish Baroque writing. In both cases the choices seem legitimate: Spain had produced vital, significant poems even before the Renaissance infusion of Petrarchan influences was nationalized by Garcilaso de la Vega and effected its sea-change in the poetry of the Iberian Peninsula. And Mexico during the time of Sor Juana was an important and powerful vice-regency and an intrinsic part of the Spanish Empire.

What I find just as incomprehensible as the appearance and disappearance of "golden ages" in cultural history is a stunning lack of familiarity in the English-speaking world with the significant poetry of the Spanish Renaissance. We pay our respects, at least in anthologies and world literature classes, to other transcendent voices, and rightly so—one cannot imagine a discussion of the European tradition without serious reference to Homer or Dante or Shakespeare—but as readers in English, our general ignorance of Spain's greatest poets is striking. It is particularly incomprehensible if one believes, as I do, that some of the esthetic pleasure we derive from literature is reflective—in other words, that art is a kind of mirror (however inaccurate, distorted, or cracked it may be) that we hold up to ourselves, looking for something approaching coherence in a welter of often chaotic and confusing experience. As we read the luminous poetry of the Spanish Golden Age, we encounter an immense number and variety of these defining, essential reflections: love, enmity, religious ecstasy, scorn, love of nature, cynicism, despair, mysticism, resignation, joy, humor: for the modern reader, it is an expressive feast of emotions and conceptualizations that nourishes our longing to make sense of our lives and our world.

When the idea of compiling and translating a collection of poems from the Spanish Golden Age was first suggested to me, I thought it important to be very clear about what I had in mind for the project. It was never my intention to create a comprehensive or scholarly anthology. By this I mean that the inclusion of one work but not another, one poet but not another, was a purely personal decision; my choices were not determined by historical or academic criteria, and I had no pretensions to all-inclusiveness; instead, my plan was to select some of my favorite poems by some of my favorite poets.

The challenge of translating these monumental works was enormous for a good number of reasons, including their overwhelming canonical stature, the inherent problem of bringing over into English a preponderantly rhymed poetry, and the difficult task of establishing criteria, no matter how personal, for selecting the poems. I had to ponder very carefully the question of how I defined the essence of a poem, how I ought to translate that essence, and how I would fulfill the translator's dual obligation to the original work and to the text in translation. I finally concluded that although separating rhyme from rhythm might well be barbarous, since rhyme is an intrinsic part of a poem's rhythmic structure, my English versions would be best served if I focused on re-creating meter.

Spanish meter is based on the number of syllables in a line, unlike English meter, which is based on the number of feet, or units composed of a stressed syllable and its satellite unstressed syllables. In preliminary versions of the translations I adhered rigidly to a syllable count per line that matched the meter in the Spanish originals until I had a framework that seemed resilient and strong; I found it fascinating that in certain poems the carefully—perhaps obsessively—imposed rhythms appeared to create their own rhymes. At this point in the translation process, after some very judicious prodding from my editor, I finally felt justified in relaxing the rules of meter when I thought the dynamic movement and flow of a line required it.

Of great concern to me was the question of major poems that had moved me deeply in the past yet which I ultimately omitted from this volume. Luis de Góngora, Francisco de Quevedo, and Sor Juana Inés de la Cruz, for example, wrote extremely long and very important poetic works of immense complexity, and I was sorely tempted to translate them—at least, to make the attempt. I finally decided, however, to confine myself for now to shorter pieces by these poets, their sonnets, in particular.

The poets included here are extraordinary figures in Spanish literature. Translating even a handful of their poems was intimidating from every conceivable point of view. Yet, at the same time, the project seemed exceedingly important to me because, once completed, it would allow contemporary readers of English access, in a single volume, to at least some of these great poems. If you already know the works, I hope these new translations do not disappoint. If the poems are new to you, then my most fervent wish is that you find in them a revelation of sheer poetic gorgeousness and profundity.

Years ago, when I was a student of Hispanic literature, my deepest passion among poets was Francisco de Quevedo, a towering writer of the seventeenth century who composed some of the most heart-wrenching yet intellectually rigorous sonnets I have ever read. After all these years and countless detours, this collection seems to have brought me back to first loves. I don't for a moment regret the journey or the return.

Edith Grossman
New York, 2006

Notes on the Poets

These notes are based on the biographical information found in standard works such as Diego Marín's *Poesía española* (New York: Las Américas, 1962) and *Lira española* (Toronto: University of Toronto, 1954), Angel del Río's *Historia de la literature española* (New York: The Dryden Press, 1948), Elias L. Rivers's *Renaissance and Baroque Poetry of Spain* (New York: Dell Publishing Co., 1966), and Arturo Torres-Ríoseco's *The Epic of Latin American Literature* (Berkeley: University of California Press, 1959).

ACKNOWLEDGMENTS

It is a pleasure for me to express my deepest gratitude to Elias L. Rivers, a great scholar and gentleman, who generously gave permission for me to use the Spanish texts included in his brilliant collection *Renaissance and Baroque Poetry of Spain*.

I also want to thank Stanko and Helen Vranich, who lent me books for the work and actually had the patience to read preliminary versions of the poems; Jaime Manrique, who, as always, brought his wonderful poetic sensibility to early readings of the translations; the copy editor Dan Shapiro; Robert Weil, an editor whose encouragement, enthusiasm, and confidence approach the super-human; and Robert Weil's assistant, Tom Mayer, whose good humor and endurance are indefatigable.

I take full responsibility for errors, misreadings, and what someone once called "lunatic misconceptions."

With the exception of Jorge Manrique's poem, for the Spanish texts of the poems I used Elias L. Rivers, *Renaissance and Baroque Poetry of Spain*, New York: Dell Publishing Co., 1966. For Manrique's *Verses* I used Janet H. Perry, *The Heath Anthology of Spanish Poetry*, Boston: D.C. Heath & Co., n.d.

THE
GOLDEN
AGE

JORGE MANRIQUE

(1440–1479)

Jorge Manrique was born into an eminent noble family and followed a military career, fighting in the armies of Fernando and Isabel, the Catholic Sovereigns, in their struggles against the feudal barons who opposed a strong centralized monarchy. He was killed in battle at the age of thirty-nine. His uncle, Gómez Manrique, was an important poet of the time, and his father, Rodrigo de Manrique, to whom *Verses Written on the Death of His Father* is dedicated, was one of the most powerful men in Spain: the Count of Paredes, Constable of Castilla, and Grand Master of the Order of Santiago.

Manrique wrote a variety of poems, most of which are considered fairly minor works, before he composed the elegy on the death of his father, in 1476, but it is this poem that established his reputation and for which he is remembered—widely, and with affection—throughout the Spanish-speaking world. Its form and themes are in no way innovative: the meter, called *pie quebrado*, or broken foot, consists of a fixed alternation of eight- and four-syllable lines in a twelve-line stanza, with a regular rhyme scheme; the traditional themes touch on the transitory nature of life on earth, an evocation of past glories in the spirit of *memento mori* (remember you must die), and an affirmation of religious belief. Despite this conventional framework, the poem's impact and significance develop from the intensity and straightforward simplicity of Manrique's poetic expression. While he influenced no school of poetry, to this day many readers of Spanish literature mention him as their favorite poet.

Coplas que fizo por la muerte de su padre

Recuerde el alma dormida,
avive el seso y despierte,
        contemplando
cómo se passa la vida,
cómo se viene la muerte
        tan callando;
cuán presto se va el plazer,
cómo después de acordado
        da dolor,
cómo a nuestro parescer,
qualquiera tiempo passado
        fué mejor.

Pues si vemos lo presente
cómo en un punto se es ido
        y acabado,
si juzgamos sabiamente,
daremos lo no venido
        por passado.
No se engañe nadie, no,
pensando que ha de durar
        lo que espera
más que duró lo que vió,
pues que todo ha de passar
        por tal manera.

Verses Written on the Death of His Father

Let the dozing soul remember,
let the mind awake and revive
    by contemplating
how our life goes by so swiftly
and how our death comes near
    so silently;
how quickly pleasure fades,
and how when it is recalled
    it gives us pain,
how we seem always to think
that times past must have been better
    than today.

If we look upon the present
and see how in a moment
    it is done,
and if we judge with wisdom
we will deem the yet-to-come
    as past and gone.
Oh, let no man be deceived
and think that what he hopes for
    will endure
longer than what has gone by,
for all things are bound to pass
    as they did before.

Nuestras vidas son los ríos
que van a dar en el mar
        que es el morir:
allí van los señoríos
derechos a se acabar
        y consumir;
allí los ríos caudales,
allí los otros, medianos
        y más chicos,
allegados son iguales,
los que viven por sus manos
        y los ricos.

    Dexo las invocaciones
de los famosos poetas
        y oradores;
no curo de sus ficciones,
que traen yervas secretas
        sus sabores.
Âquel solo me encomiendo,
âquel solo invoco yo
        de verdad,
que en este mundo viviendo,
el mundo no conosció
        su deidad.

Our lives are the rivers
that empty into the sea
        that is our dying:
there flow great lords and high princes
directly to their ending
        to be consumed;
there flow the mightiest rivers,
and the others, tributaries
        and lesser streams,
joined together and equal
are those who live by their labor
        and wealthy men.

I forsake the invocations
of orators most renowned
        and famed bards;
I leave behind their fictions,
for those delights bear in them
        hidden simples;
I trust solely in the One,
I invoke solely the One
        Who, in truth,
though living here in the world
the world did not acknowledge
        Him as God.

Este mundo es el camino
para el otro, que es morada
        sin pesar;
mas cumple tener buen tino
para andar esta jornada
        sin errar.
Partimos cuando nascemos,
andamos mientras vivimos,
        y llegamos
al tiempo que fenescemos;
assí que quando morimos
        descansamos.

Este mundo bueno fué
si bien usássemos dél
        como devemos,
porque, según nuestra fe,
es para ganar aquel
        que atendemos.
Y aun aquel fijo de Dios
para sobirnos al cielo
        descendió
a nascer acá entre nos,
y a vivir en este suelo
        do murió.

This world of ours is the pathway
that leads us to the next, our
        heavenly home;
but one must have good judgment
to travel along this road
        and not to err.
We set out when we are born,
we walk while we are alive,
        and we arrive
at the moment that we pass;
and so, when at last we die
        we come to rest.

This world possesses virtue
if we use it as wisely
        as we ought,
because, as our faith teaches,
passage to the next should be
        our sole concern.
And even the Son of God,
to raise us up to heaven,
        made His descent
to be born here among us,
and to live here on this earth
        and meet His death.

Si fuesse en nuestro poder
tornar la cara fermosa
    corporal,
como podemos fazer
el ánima gloriósa
    angelical,
¡qué diligencia tan viva
tovieramos toda hora,
    y tan presta,
en componer la cativa,
dexándonos la señora
    descompuesta!

Ved de quán poco valor
son las cosas tras que andamos
    y corremos,
que, en este mundo traidor,
aun primero que muramos
    las perdemos:
dellas desfaze la edad,
dellas casos desastrados
    que acaescen,
dellas, por su calidad,
en los más altos estados
    desfallescen.

If it lay within our power
to make our corporal face
        as beautiful
as our glorious soul when made
        angelical,
what diligence, what persistence
we would bring so constantly,
        so willingly,
to remedy what is foul,
and leave our homely visage
        utterly changed!

See what little value
lies in the things we strive for
        and pursue,
for in this world of deceit,
even before we perish
        they are lost;
age and time destroy them,
the most awful disasters
        befall them,
and by their very nature,
they perish when they reach their
        highest state.

Dezidme, la fermosura,
la gentil frescura y tez
    de la cara,
la color y la blancura,
quando viene la vejez,
    ¿quál se para?
Las mañas y ligereza
y la fuerça corporal
    de joventud,
todo se torna graveza
quando llega al arrabal
    de senectud.

    Pues la sangre de los godos,
y el linaje, y la nobleza
    tan crescida,
¡por quántas vías y modos
se sume su grand alteza
    en esta vida!
Unos, por poco valer,

Tell me: one's beauty, one's charm,
the lovely, fresh complexion
    of one's face,
its color, creamy and pale,
when old age comes as it must,
    where are they?
The agility and speed,
the bodily strength and vigor
    of one's youth,
they all turn heavy and dense
when entering the sullen precincts
    of old age.

    The ancient blood of the Goths[1]
the highest and most noble
    lineages,
in how many ways and forms
do men exalt that grandeur
    in this life!
Yet some who do not prize them,

[1]The Visigoths, who ruled Spain from roughly the fourth to the eight centuries, were generally considered to be the Christian ancestors of the noblest Spaniards. This was probably the consequence of the division of the Iberian Peninsula into a Christian north and a Muslim south during the Middle Ages.

¡por quán baxos y abatidos
　　que los tienen!
Y otros, por no tener,
con oficios no devidos
　　se mantienen.

　　Los estados y riqueza,
que nos dexan a desora,
　　¿quién lo duda?
No les pidamos firmeza,
pues son de una señora
　　que se muda;
que bienes son de Fortuna
que revuelve con su rueda
　　presurosa,
la qual no puede ser una,
ni estar estable ni queda
　　en una cosa.

　　Pero digo que acompañen
y lleguen hasta la huessa
　　con su duéño:
por esso no nos engañen,

despise them and judge them low
    and without worth!
Others, who do not have them,
follow vile and base pursuits
    to survive.

    Position, power, and treasure
abandon us when they will,
    none can doubt it.
Do not ask them to be steadfast,
for they belong to a Lady[2]
    ruled by caprice;
they are the goods of Fortune
who turns around completely
    with her wheel,
and cannot be firm and true
or everlasting, or fixed
    on just one thing.

    But I say these goods follow us,
that they go straight to the grave
    with their owner:
let us never be deceived,

[2]The traditional image is of Dame Fortune (in modern terms, Lady Luck) capriciously spinning her wheel so that the high and low exchange places.

pues se va la vida apriessa
          como sueño.
Y los deleites de acá
son, en que nos deleitamos,
          temporales,
y los tormentos de allá,
que por ellos esperamos,
          eternales.

     Los plazeres y dulçores
desta vida trabajada
          que tenemos,
¿qué son sino corredores,
y la muerte la celada
          en que caemos?
No mirando nuestro daño,
corremos a rienda suelta
          sin parar;
desque vemos el engaño
y queremos dar la vuelta,
          no hay lugar.

     Essos reyes poderosos
que vemos por escrituras
          ya passadas,
con casos tristes llorosos

for life goes by as quickly
　　as a dream;
and the pleasures we have here
and in which we take delight,
　　they are passing,
and the torments far below,
the torments that await us
　　last forever.

　The pleasant joys, the contentments
of the glittering grand life that
　　we live here,
what are they but speeding racers
and death the snare, the ambush
　　where we fall?
Not thinking of traps, of danger,
　　we run as fast as we can,
　　without pause;
but when we see the deception
and want to change our course, it
　　is too late.

　Those mighty kings and rulers
who fill the histories of
　　times long past,
all their good fortune, their greatness,

fueron sus buenas venturas
        trastornadas;
assí que no hay cosa fuerte,
que a papas y emperadores
        y prelados
assí los trata la Muerte
como a los pobres pastores
        de ganados. . . .

        ¿Qué se fizo el rey don Juan?
Los infantes de Aragón,
        ¿qué se fizieron?
¿Qué fué de tanto galán?
¿Qué fué de tanta invención
        como truxieron?
Las justas y los torneos,
paramentos, bordaduras,
        y cimeras,
¿fueron sino devaneos?
¿qué fueron sino verduras
        de las eras?

were transformed into piteous
    mournful states;
there is nothing that endures,
for great popes and famed emperors
    and high prelates
are treated by Death as harshly
as she treats the humblest shepherd
    or tender of flocks. . . .

    Where now is the king Don Juan?[3]
And the princes of Aragon,[4]
    where are they?
What happened to their gallantry?
What happened to all they imagined
    and devised?
Their tourneys and jousts so brave,
their embellishments, adornments,
    and their crests,
what were they but idle folly?
What were they but leavings on the
    threshing floor?

[3]King Juan II of Castile, an important patron of the arts in the fifteenth century.
[4]The sons of Fernando de Antequera, king of Aragon in the late-fourteenth and early-fifteenth centuries.

¿Qué se fizieron las damas,
sus tocados, sus vestidos,
   sus olores?
¿Qué se fizieron las llamas
de los fuegos encendidos
   de amadores?
¿Qué se fizo aquel trobar,
las músicas acordadas
   que tañían?
¿Qué se fizo aquel dançar,
aquellas ropas chapadas
   que traían?

Pues el otro su heredero,
don Enrique, ¡qué poderes
   alcançava!
¡Quán blando, quán falaguero
el mundo con sus plazeres
   se le dava!
Mas veréts quán enemigo,
quán contrario, quán cruel
   se le mostró,

Where now are the beauteous ladies,
their headdresses and their gowns,
        their sweet perfumes?
Where now are the ardent flames,
the fires of high passion
        by lovers lit?
Where now their fair versifying
and the harmonies of music
        that they played?
Where now their graceful dancing,
and the clothing, fine and flowing,
        that they wore?

    And that other king, his heir,
Don Enrique,[5] what great power
        he achieved!
How tender and how benign
the world and all its pleasures
        seemed to him!
But you will see what animus,
what enmity, what cruelty
        the world displayed,

[5]Enrique IV, a king of Castile in the fifteenth century, was symbolically deposed in 1465 and lived in wretched poverty until his death in 1474.

aviéndole sido amigo,
¡quán poco duró con él
    lo que le dió!

    Las dádivas desmedidas,
los edificios reales
    llenos de oro,
las vaxillas tan febridas,
los enriques y reales
    del tesoro,
los jaezes, los cavallos
de su gente, y atavíos
    tan sobrados,
¿dónde iremos a buscallos?
¿qué fueron sino rocíos
    de los prados? . . .

    Pues aquel grand condestable,
maestre que conoscimos
    tan privado,
no cumple que dél se fable,
sino sólo que lo vimos
    degollado.

for it had been his friend, yet
how briefly all it gave him
    did endure!

    The extravagant, splendid gifts,
the palaces, the royal dwellings
    filled with gold,
the resplendent table settings,
the treasure, gold and silver,
    in the coffers,
the rich trappings and the horses
of his courtiers, their splendid
    finery,
where shall we go to find them?
What were they but fleeting dewdrops
    in the fields? . . .

    And that great High Constable,[6]
commander and noble favorite,
    whom we knew,
we ought not speak of him,
but we will say that we witnessed
    his beheading.

[6]Don Álvaro de Luna, the Constable of Castile, was the favorite of Juan II, but he fell into disgrace and was beheaded in 1453.

Sus infinitos tesoros,
sus villas y sus lugares,
        su mandar,
¿qué le fueron sino lloros?
¿fuéronle sino pesares
        al dexar? . . .

    Aquel de buenos abrigo,
amado por virtuoso
        de la gente,
el maestre don Rodrigo
Manrique, tanto famoso
        y tan valiente,
sus grandes fechos y claros
no cumple que los alabe,
        pues los vieron,
no los quiero fazer caros,
pues el mundo todo sabe
        quáles fueron.

    ¡Qué amigo de sus amigos!
¡Qué señor para criados
        y parientes!
¡Qué enemigo de enemigos!

His vast wealth and immense domains,
his villages and estates,
        his command,
what were they to him but grief?
What were they but pain and sorrow
        when he left them? . . .

    He who was shelter to the good,
beloved for his many virtues
        by all people,
the commander Don Rodrigo
Manrique,[7] a man so famed
        and so valiant,
that his brave, illustrious deeds—
we ought not to praise them, for
        each was seen—
I do not wish to exalt them,
for every person living knows
        what those deeds were.

    What a friend he was to friends!
What a master to his servants
        and his kin!
What a foe he was to foes!

[7]Jorge Manrique's father, to whom this poem is dedicated.

¡Qué maestro de esforçados
    y valientes!
¡Qué seso para discretos!
¡Qué gracia para donosos!
      ¡Qué razón!
¡Qué benigno a los subjetos,
y a los bravos y dañosos,
    un león! . . .

  No dexó grandes tesoros,
ni alcançó grandes riquezas
    ni vaxillas,
mas fizo guerra a los moros,
ganando sus fortalezas
    y sus villas;
y en las lides que venció,
muchos moros y cavallos
    se perdieron,
y en este oficio ganó
las rentas y los vassallos
    que le dieron. . . .

What a teacher to the brave
    and valorous!
What intelligence for the wise!
What wit for the elegant!
    And what reason!
What benevolence for subjects,
and to the wild and unruly,
    what a lion. . . .

He did not leave vast treasure,
he did not achieve great riches,
    immense wealth,
but he waged war against Moors,[8]
conquering their citadels
    and estates;
and in the battles he won,
countless Moors and their horses
    were cut down,
and in this endeavor he gained
the income, rents and vassals
    that passed to him. . . .

[8]The Moors, North African Muslims, invaded the Iberian Peninsula in 711. In the centuries that followed, Christian forces engaged them in countless wars and battles until the Moors' final defeat by Fernando of Aragon and Isabel of Castile in 1492.

Después de puesta la vida
tantas vezes por su ley
    al tablero,
después de tan bien servida
la corona de su rey
    verdadero,
después de tanta hazaña
a que no puede bastar
    cuenta cierta,
en la su villa de Ocaña
vino la Muerte a llamar
    a su puerta,

    diziendo:—"Buen cavallero,
dexad el mundo engañoso
    y su halago:
vuestro corazón de azero
muestre su esfuerço famoso
    en este trago;
y pues de vida y salud

After having risked his life
so many times in the cause of
    loyalty,
after having served so well
the crown and scepter of his
    one true king,[9]
after his memorable feats,
his memorable deeds, too many
    to recount,
on his estate in Ocaña[10]
Death came for him, Death came knocking
    on his door,

    saying: "Hear me, virtuous knight,
leave behind the deceptive world,
    its pleasures false:
let your heart be strong as steel
and show its valor and courage
    in this sore trial;
for you once cared very little

[9]He supported Fernando and Isabel in their struggles against the feudal barons who resisted their effort to unify their kingdoms and establish a centralized monarchy.
    [10]Located in the province of Toledo, in Castile.

fezistes tan poca cuenta
         por la fama,
esfuérçese la virtud
para sofrir esta afruenta
         que vos llama.

   "No se os faga tan amarga
la batalla temerosa
         que esperáis,
pues otra vida más larga
de fama tan gloriosa
         acá dexáis.
Aunque esta vida de onor
tampoco no es eternal
         ni verdadera,
mas con todo es muy mejor
que la otra temporal
         perescedera.

   "El vivir que es perdurable
no se gana con estados
         mundanales,
ni con vida deleitable,
en que moran los pecados
         infernales;
mas los buenos religiosos

for life and health in your quest
        for knightly fame,
call on that virtue now, and you
will endure the somber blow
        that summons you.

    "Do not think of it as bitter,
the dreadful, dire battle
        that awaits you,
for another, more lasting life
of glorious, well-earned fame
        you leave behind you.
And though honor and renown
are not the life eternal,
        the one true life,
yet they are better by far
than man's other, earthly life
        that perishes.

    "The true, the enduring life
is not won with the high rank
        of this world,
or with a life of pleasures
and all the deadly sins
        that dwell within;
it is won by pious men with

gánanlo con oraciones
        y con lloros,
los cavalleros famosos
con trabajos y aflicciones
        contra moros.

    "Y pues vos, claro varón,
tanta sangre derramastes
        de paganos,
esperad el galardón
que en este mundo ganastes
        por las manos;
y con esta confiança,
y con la fe tan entera
        que tenéis,
partid con buena esperança,
que estotra vida tercera
        ganaréis."

    —"No gastemos tiempo ya
en esta vida mezquina
        por tal modo,
que mi voluntad está
conforme con la divina
        para todo;
y consiento en mi morir

their prayers and supplications,
        their lamentations,
and by famed knights and warriors
with suffering in their struggles
        against the Moors.

    "And you, illustrious noble,
having shed so great a torrent
        of heathen blood,
can look forward to the reward
you earned here in the world with
        your own hands;
and with this firm confidence,
and with the sure, unshaken faith
        that is yours,
depart with the certain hope
that you will win that eternal,
        that third life."

    "Now let us spend no more time
on this miserable, this worthless
        mortal life,
for in everything my will
conforms with the divine will,
        the will of God;
and I consent to my dying

con voluntad plazentera
    clara y pura,
que querer ombre vivir
quando Dios quiere que muera
    es locura.

"Tú, que por nuestra maldad
tomaste forma servil
    y baxo nombre,
Tú, que a tu divinidad
juntaste cosa tan vil
    como el ombre,
Tú, que tan grandes tormentos
sofriste sin resistencia
    en tu persona,
no por mis merescimientos,
mas por tu sola clemencia
    me perdona."

Assí con tal entender,
todos sentidos umanos
    conservados,
cercado de su muger,
de sus fijos y hermanos
    y criados,
dió el alma a quien gela dió,

and submit to a desire
        bright and pure;
it is madness for a man
to wish to live when God wishes
        him to die.

    "You, who because of our sins
took on a lowly form and
        a base name,
who joined to your nature divine
a thing as paltry and vile
        as is man,
You, who suffered torments so cruel,
not resisting or demurring
        in Your person,
not on account of my merits,
only because of Your mercy,
        Oh, forgive me."

    And so with this understanding,
and with all his human senses
        still preserved,
surrounded by his dear wife,
his children, brothers, sisters,
        and his servants,
he gave up his soul to the One

el qual la ponga en el cielo
    en su gloria,
y aunque la vida murió
nos dexó harto consuelo
    su memoria.

who gave it to him; may He
    return it to
heaven's glory. Though he is dead,
his memory lives on to
    comfort us.

GARCILASO DE LA VEGA

(1501?–1536)

Garcilaso de la Vega was born in Toledo into a high-ranking, noble family. Serving as courtier and warrior in the court of Charles V, he followed a military career in the service of the king but fell out of favor at court and, in 1531, was sent into exile, initially to an island in the Danube. Later he went to Naples, which was under Spanish rule and where he remained until nearly the end of his life in the service of the viceroy, a member of the house of the Duke of Alba. He was killed in an attack on the Muey castle, in Provence.

Garcilaso's immense reputation as a poetic innovator is based on his adoption and nationalization of Petrarchan forms, in particular, the sonnet and the hendecasyllable, or eleven-syllable line. Other poets in Spain had used Italianate meters before him—for example, the Marqués de Santillana in the fifteenth century, and Garcilaso's close friend and comrade-in-arms, Juan de Boscán, who encouraged him to experiment with Petrarchan meters and who wrote Italianate verse as well. Garcilaso, however, was the poet who perfected them in Spanish, achieving a natural fluidity and conveying what came to be seen as a Renaissance sensibility in his evocations of sensuous love and nature's beauty.

Garcilaso nationalized the Petrarchan esthetic so successfully that, during the Renaissance, Italianate meters and attitudes came to seem native to Spain. "Lyre," for example, the last word of the first line in his "Song V," lent its name to the fixed alternation of regularly rhymed eleven- and seven-syllable lines in which the poem was written; later in the sixteenth century, this meter became a favorite form of Fray Luis de León (see p. 101) and San Juan de la Cruz (see p. 125). Boscán collected and preserved Garcilaso's poems— three eclogues, a handful of elegies and odes, and some thirty sonnets. They were first published, along with the poems of Boscán, in 1543 by Boscán's widow; they circulated widely, became very popular, and were frequently edited, annotated, and republished throughout the sixteenth and seventeenth centuries.

Soneto I

Cuando me paro a contemplar mi estado,
y a ver los pasos por do me ha traído,
hallo, según por do anduve perdido,
que a mayor mal pudiera haber llegado;

mas cuando del camino estó olvidado,
a tanto mal no sé por dó he venido;
sé que me acabo, y más he yo sentido
ver acabar conmigo mi cuidado.

Yo acabaré, que me entregué sin arte
a quien sabrá perderme y acabarme
si ella quisiere, y aun sabrá querello;

que pues mi voluntad puede matarme,
la suya, que no es tanto de mi parte,
pudiendo, ¿qué hará sino hacello?

Sonnet I

When I stand and contemplate my state,
and look back at the path that brought me here,
I find, in light of how I lost my way,
I might have met a much more bitter fate;
    if I ignore my steps along that road,
then I know not just how I came to grief;
I know my life is over, and I rue
the passing of my sorrow when I die.
    I shall meet my end, for I gave my heart
to one who could destroy and ruin me
if she should wish, and she could learn to wish;
    for if my will can bring about my death,
hers, less partial to my cause, will kill me
if it can, and why should it refrain?

Soneto X

¡Oh dulces prendas, por mi mal halladas,
dulces y alegres cuando Dios quería!
Juntas estáis en la memoria mía,
y con ella en mi muerte conjuradas.

¿Quién me dijera, cuando en las pasadas
horas en tanto bien por vos me vía,
que me habíades de ser en algún día
con tan grave dolor representadas?

Pues en un hora junto me llevastes
todo el bien que por términos me distes,
llevadme junto el mal que me dejastes;

si no, sospecharé que me pusistes
en tantos bienes porque deseastes
verme morir entre memorias tristes.

Sonnet X

O sweet mementoes, to my sorrow found,
so dear and joyous when it was God's will!
Joined forever in memory and mind,
together you conspire to see my death.

No one could have told me in times long past,
when you and you alone brought so much joy,
that on a bitter day you'd come back to me
in the bleak company of so much grief.

Since in one hour you have taken from me
the joys doled out a little at a time,
take from me too the sorrow left behind;

if you do not, I cannot but believe
you brought me joy only because you wished
to see me die of memories filled with grief.

Soneto XXIII

En tanto que de rosa y azucena
se muestra la color en vuestro gesto,
y que vuestro mirar ardiente, honesto,
enciende al corazón y lo refrena;

y en tanto que el cabello, que en la vena
del oro se escogió, con vuelo presto,
por el hermoso cuello blanco, enhiesto,
el viento mueve, esparce y desordena:

coged de vuestra alegre primavera
el dulce fruto, antes que el tiempo airado
cubra de nieve la hermosa cumbre.

Marchitará la rosa el viento helado,
todo lo mudará la edad ligera
por no hacer mudanza en su costumbre.

Sonnet XXIII

For as long as the lily and the rose
give their color and hue to your fair face,
and the look in your eyes, ardent and chaste,
inflames my heart and yet restrains it too;
    and for as long as your hair, taken from veins
of purest gold, shimmers around your throat
—so beautiful, so slender, and so white—
blown in disarray by the gentle breeze:
    oh gather, in the joy of this your spring
the sweetest fruit before a sullen time
covers that gleaming mountaintop with snow.
    The icy wind will wither the fair rose,
fleet-footed age will change and transform all
but never alter its own ancient ways.

Soneto XXIX

Pasando el mar Leandro el animoso,
en amoroso fuego todo ardiendo,
esforzó el viento, y fuése embraveciendo
el agua con un ímpetu furioso.
    Vencido del trabajo presuroso,
contrastar a las ondas no pudiendo,
y más del bien que allí perdía muriendo
que de su propia vida congojoso,
    como pudo esforzó su voz cansada
y a las ondas habló desta manera,
mas nunca fuéla voz dellas oída:
    —Ondas, pues no se escusa que yo muera,
dejadme allá llegar, es y a la tornada
vuestro furor esecutá en mi vida.—

Sonnet XXIX

Brave Leander,[1] dauntless, crossing the sea,
on fire with the blazing flames of love,
when winds blew strong and waters rose and swirled
with frenzied rage and driving, crashing swells.
   Vanquished by struggle, nearly overcome,
he could no longer battle with the waves,
and dying because of the love he'd lose
and not because his own life ebbed away, ·
   he raised his weary voice and faintly called,
speaking his final words to roiling waves,
but they ne'er heard his voice, his lover's plea:
   "Waves, I know I cannot escape my death,
but let me swim across; when I return
you can vent your wrathful surge upon my life."

[1]In Greek mythology, Leander swam the Hellespont—known in modern times as the Dardanelles—every night to visit Hero. One night he drowned, and Hero, in despair, threw herself into the ocean.

Canción V

Si de mi baja lira
tanto pudiese el son, que un momento
aplacase la ira
del animoso viento,
y la furia del mar y el movimiento,

y en ásperas montañas
con el suave canto enterneciese
las fieras alimañas,
los árboles moviese,
y al son confusamente los trajese:

no pienses que cantado
sería de mí, hermosa flor de Nido,
el fiero Marte airado,
a muerte convertido,
de polvo y sangre y de sudor teñido,

Song V

If this my humble lyre[1]
produced a sound that in a single moment
appeased and soothed the ire
of the fiercely blowing wind,
and the furious turmoil of the sea,

    and in the untamed mountains
it could lull and soften with gentle song
ferocious, ravening beasts
and move the stalwart trees,
and draw them, in confusion, toward the sound:

    oh, do not think, fair flower
of Gnido,[2] that I would ever sing that song
to savage, wrathful Mars,[3]
fixed forever on death
and stained with dust and blood, and streaked with sweat,

[1]The opening of the poem recalls the Greek myth of Orpheus, who played
Apollo's lyre and charmed everyone—and everything—that heard him.
    [2]Gnido, a district in Naples, is home to the lady (the "fair flower") whom
Garcilaso addresses in the poem.
    [3]Mars is the Roman god of war.

ni aquellos capitanes
en las sublimes ruedas colocados,
por quien los alemanes,
el fiero cuello atados,
y los franceses van domesticados;

mas solamente aquella
fuerza de tu beldad sería cantada,
y alguna vez con ella
también sería notada
el aspereza de que estás armada,

y cómo por ti sola,
y por tu gran valor y hermosura,
convertido en vïola,
llora su desventura
el miserable amante en su figura.

Hablo de aquel cativo
de quien tener se debe más cuidado,
que está muriendo vivo,

or sing to valiant captains
placed in honor on chariots sublime,
leading the vanquished German
bound by his barbarous neck,
and the captive Frenchman, tamed now, subdued;[4]

but I would only sing
to the unconquered power of your fair face,
and then, along with praise,
I'd take some passing note
of the cruel weapons you wield, those dire arms,

and how, because of you
and your great beauty and your noble worth,
a woeful lover, transformed,
and weakened like tattered blossoms,
laments his deep misfortune, shedding tears.

I speak of that poor captive
—much greater care surely should attend him—
whose life is living death,

[4]The references are to peoples defeated by Rome and brought back in triumph by the victorious generals.

al remo condenado,
en la concha de Venus amarrado.

Por ti, como solía,
del áspero caballo no corrige
la furia y gallardía:
ni con freno le rige,
ni con vivas espuelas ya le aflige.

Por ti, con diestra mano
no revuelve la espada presurosa,
y en el dudoso llano
huye la polvorosa
palestra como sierpe ponzoñosa.

Por ti, su blanda musa,
en lugar de la cítara sonante,

condemned as a galley slave,[5]
and chained and shackled in the shell of Venus.[6]

Because of you he no longer
controls and rules the fury, the high spirits
of a wild steed untamed,
or governs its path with the bit,
or disciplines with the merest touch of spurs.[7]

Because of you his hand, once deft,
no longer wields a swiftly flashing sword,
and on the doubtful plain
he flees the dust of combat
as if it were a venomous fanged snake.

Because of you, tender muse,
instead of the dulcet lute's sonorities

[5]From earliest times, and until the practice was abolished during the French Revolution, convicted criminals throughout the Mediterranean could be sent to serve as oarsmen on a galley, a ship powered by both oars and sails. Depending upon the length of their penal servitude, this could be tantamount to a death sentence.

[6]Venus, the Roman goddess of love, was born of sea-foam, and rose to the surface of the ocean in a seashell.

[7]This is the work of a warrior; in other words, the lover has lost his knightly skills.

tristes querellas usa,
que con llanto abundante
hacen bañar el rostro del amante.

Por ti, el mayor amigo
le es importuno, grave y enojoso;
yo puedo ser testigo,
que ya del peligroso
naufragio fuí su puerto y su reposo;

y agora en tal manera
vence el dolor a la razón perdida,
que ponzoñosa fiera
nunca fué aborrecida
tanto como yo dél, ni tan temida.

No fuiste tú engendrada
ni producida de la dura tierra;
no debe ser notada
que ingratamente yerra
quien todo el otro error de sí destierra.

he plays dolorous laments
that bathe the lover's face
with flowing streams of his abundant tears.

  Because of you, his greatest friend
now is tiresome, intrusive, tedious;
to this I can bear witness
who once was his safe haven
from the dangers of shipwreck on rough seas;

  but now his grief entirely
overshadows the reason he has lost,
no poisonous, gruesome beast
was ever so despised
as I am scorned by him, and even feared.

  Oh, you were not engendered
nor born of obstinate, insensate earth;
she who forswears and forbids
all error should not be known
as one whom ingratitude has led astray.

Hágate temerosa
el caso de Anajérete, y cobarde,
que de ser desdeñosa
se arrepintió muy tarde;
y así, su alma con su mármol arde.

Estábase alegrando
del mal ajeno el pecho empedernido,
cuando abajo mirando,
el cuerpo muerto vido
del miserable amante, allí tendido,

y al cuello el lazo atado,
con que desenlazó de la cadena
el corazón cuitado,
que con su breve pena
compró la eterna punición ajena.

Sintió allí convertirse
en piedad amorosa el aspereza.
¡Oh tarde arrepentirse!

The fate of Anaxarete[8]
should be a warning; it should give you pause,
for too late she repented
of her disdain and scorn,
and so, encased in marble, her soul burns.

Cruelly, in her heart of flint,
she was rejoicing at another's grief
when, glancing down, she saw
the body, hushed and cold,
of her lover lying dead at her feet,

and still round his neck the rope
he used to free from shackles, bonds, and chains
his mournful, wounded heart,
and with his short-lived pain
he bought another's eternal punishment.

Then and there she felt transformed,
her harshness became a loving sympathy.
Oh, repentance come too late!

[8]In Greek mythology, Anaxarete treated her lover, Iphus, so cruelly that he
hanged himself above her door. She remained indifferent to his fate and was
turned by Aphrodite, the Greek goddess of love, into a statue.

¡Oh última terneza!
¿Cómo te sucedió mayor dureza?

   Los ojos se enclavaron
en el tendido cuerpo que alli vieron;
los huesos se tornaron
más duros y crecieron,
y en sí toda la carne convirtieron;

   las entrañas heladas
tornaron poco a poco en piedra dura;
por las venas cuitadas
la sangre su figura
iba desconociendo y su natura;

   hasta que, finalmente,
en duro mármol vuelta y trasformada,
hizo de sí la gente
no tan maravillada
cuanto de aquella ingratitude vengada.

   No quieras tú, señora,
de Némesis airada las saetas
probar, por Dios, agora;

Oh, final glint of gentleness!
How could a greater hardness e'er replace you?

    Her eyes stared, fixed upon
the outstretched body they saw lying there;
her bones turned even harder
and grew till they transformed
all the flesh of her body into bone;

    her icy, frozen organs
turned little by little into obdurate stone;
and in the agonized veins
her blood no longer knew
itself, its form and nature, as it changed;

    until, at last, in the end,
transformed forever into dense, cold marble,
those near her, those who saw,
felt not so much astonished
as avenged for her severe ingratitude.

    O lady, for God's sake
do not try now to test the deadly arrows
of Nemesis[9] the wrathful;

[9]Among other things, the Greek goddess Nemesis punished crimes.

baste que tus perfetas
obras y hermosura a los poetas

    den inmortal materia,
sin que también en verso lamentable
celebren la miseria
de algún caso notable
que por ti pase, triste y miserable.

let it be enough that your
perfect acts and beauty give to poets

   immortal subjects and themes;
do not allow them, in verses of lament,
to celebrate the sorrow
of some famed catastrophe
brought on by you, so wretched and so sad.

Égloga I

El dulce lamentar de dos pastores,
Salicio juntamente y Nemoroso,
he de contra, sus quejas imitando;
cuyas ovejas al cantar sabroso
estaban muy atentas, los amores,
de pacer olvidadas, escuchando.
Tú, que ganaste obrando
un nombre en todo el mundo
y un grado sin segundo,
agora estés atento sólo y dado
al ínclito gobierno del Estado
Albano; agora vuelto a la otra parte,
resplandeciente, armado,
representando en tierra el fiero Marte;
agora de cuidados enojosos
y de negocios libre, por ventura
andes a caza, el monte fatigando
en ardiente jinete, que apresura
el curso tras los ciervos temerosos,
que en vano su morir van dilatando:
espera, que en tornando
a ser restitüdo
al ocio ya perdido,

Eclogue I

    The dulcet lamentation of two shepherds,
one named Salicio, th'other Nemoroso,[1]
I shall tell, imitating their laments;
their sheep paid heed to their sweet songs, forgetting
to graze, listening to their plaints of love.
You,[2] whose great deeds have won you
renown throughout the world
and unrivaled rank and title,
whether you now are tending only to
the famed, noble governance of the Alban
State,[3] or are turned elsewhere, to other feats,
resplendent in full armor,
representing warlike Mars here on earth;
or free of the heavy burden of affairs,
perhaps at the hunt, tearing through the woods
on a fiery steed racing at a gallop
after the deer, terrified, full of fear,
that attempt in vain to postpone their deaths:
wait, when I return again
to serenity now lost,

---

[1]Salicio and Nemoroso are names traditionally associated with pastoral literature.

[2]The poet addresses Don Pedro de Toledo, viceroy of Naples.

[3]Don Pedro was a member of the ducal house of Alba; the reference is to Naples.

luego verás ejercitar mi pluma
por la infinita innumerable suma
de tus virtudes y famosas obras,
antes que me consuma,
faltando a ti, que a todo el mundo sobras.

    En tanto que este tiempo que adivino
viene a sacarme de la deuda, un día,
que se debe a tu fama y a tu gloria
(que es deuda general, no sólo mía,
mas de cualquier ingenio peregrino
que celebra lo dino de memoria),
el árbol de vitoria
que ciñe estrechamente
tu glorïosa frente
dé lugar a la hiedra que se planta
debajo de tu sombra, y se levanta
poco a poco, arrimada a tus loores;
y en cuanto esto se canta,
escucha tú el cantar de mis pastores.

    Saliendo de las ondas encendido,
rayaba de los montes el altura
el sol, cuando Salicio, recostado
al pie de un alta haya en la verdura,
por donde un agua clara con sonido
atravesaba el fresco y verde prado,
él, con canto acordado

then you will see my pen at once engaged,
before I meet my death,
in telling the tale without end
of all your virtues, all your famous deeds,
for I've neglected you, greater than the rest.

   And while the time that I foresee draws near
to relieve me, one day, of this heavy debt
owed to your great glory and your fame
(it is a general debt, not mine alone,
but belonging to all rare and gifted minds
that celebrate what's worthy of remembrance),
may the wreath of victory
that so closely encircles
your noble, glorious brow
give way to leaves of ivy sown in your shade,
a planted vine that little by little climbs,
leaning on and clinging to praise of you;
and till that song is sung,
I beg you, hear the singing of my shepherds.

   The sun rose fiery red, up from the waves,
its rays shone on the lofty mountain peaks
when Salicio, reclining on the grass
verdant at the foot of a lofty beech,
near where a sounding brook of crystal water
passed through the pleasant meadow, fresh and green,
began his song in harmony

al rumor que sonaba,
del agua que pasaba,
se quejaba tan dulce y blandamente
como si no estuviera de allí ausente
la que de su dolor culpa tenía;
y así, como presente,
razonando con ella, le decía:

Salicio
    ¡Oh más dura que mármol a mis quejas,
y al encendido fuego en que me quemo
más helada que nieve, Galatea!,
estoy muriendo, y aún la vida temo;
témola con razón, pues tú me dejas,
que no hay, sin ti, el vivir para qué sea.
Vergüenza he que me vea
ninguno en tal estado,
de ti desamparado,
y de mí mismo yo me corro agora.
¿De un alma te desdeñas ser señora,
donde siempre moraste, no pudiendo
della salir un hora?
Salid sin duelo, lágrimas, corriendo.
    El sol tiende los rayos de su lumbre

with the gentle murmur of
the stream as it passed him by,
lamenting in a voice so sweet and soft
that she who was to blame for his deep sorrow
seemed not to be away, absent from him;
and addressing her as if
she were present, he spoke to her and said:

Salicio
    Much harder than marble to my complaints,
and to the blazing fire in which I burn,
O Galatea,[4] colder than the snow!
I die, and even so, still I fear life;
I am right to fear it, for you are leaving,
and with you gone, I have no reason to live.
It would fill me with shame
if any saw me like this,
alone, abandoned by you,
and I am mortified at my own state.
Do you scorn being mistress of a soul
where you once always dwelled, not able even
to leave it for an hour?
Ah, flow, my tears, stream forth without remorse.
    The sun sends its brilliant flames of light

[4]Galatea is a name associated with the pastoral tradition.

por montes y por valles, despertando
las aves y animales y la gente:
cuál por el aire claro va volando,
cuál por el verde valle o alta cumbre
paciendo va segura y libremente,
cuál con el sol presente
va de nuevo al oficio,
y al usado ejercicio
do su natura o menester le inclina:
siempre está en llanto esta ánima mezquina,
cuando la sombra el mundo va cubriendo
o la luz se avecina.
Salid sin duelo, lágrimas, corriendo.

¿Y tú desta mi vida ya olvidada,
sin mostrar un pequeño sentimiento
de que por ti Salicio triste muera,
dejas llevar, desconocida, al viento
el amor y la fe que ser guardada
eternamente sólo a mí debiera?
¡Oh Dios!, ¿por qué siquiera,
pues ves desde tu altura
esta falsa perjura
causar la muerte de un estrecho amigo,
no recibe del cielo algún castigo?
Si en pago del amor yo estoy muriendo,
¿qué hará el enemigo?

along mountains and into valleys, waking
the birds and animals, and waking people:
some go flying through air so clear and bright,
some in green valleys or on mountain peaks
go grazing, wandering safely, and free,
and some, with the rising sun
again go to their labor,
to the customary toil
that their nature or need inclines them to:
but this my wretched soul is always weeping,
when dark night and shadows cover the earth
or when the light draws near.
Ah, flow, my tears, stream forth without remorse.

    And you, forgetful now of this my life,
showing no sorrow, not the least regret
for sad Salicio, dying for your sake,
ungrateful one, do you allow the wind
to carry away the love and faith that you
should have kept for me alone, eternally?
O God! You see from on high
how false she is, a traitor,
causing the death of a friend;
if You see, then tell me why Heaven does not
condemn her to the punishment she deserves.
If death is my reward for loving her,
what becomes of her enemy?

Salid sin duelo, lágrimas, corriendo.

    Por ti el silencio de la selva umbrosa,
por ti la esquividad y apartamiento
del solitario monte me agradaba;
por ti la verde hierba, el fresco viento,
el blanco lirio y colorada rosa
y dulce primavera deseaba.
¡Ay, cuánto me engañaba!
¡Ay, cuán diferente era
y cuán de otra manera
lo que en tu falso pecho se escondía!
Bien claro con su voz me lo decía
la siniestra corneja, repitiendo
la desventura mía.
Salid sin duelo, lágrimas, corriendo.

    ¡Cuántas veces, durmiendo en la floresta,
reputándolo yo por desvarío,
vi mi mal entre sueños, desdichado!
Soñaba que en el tiempo del estío
llevaba, por pasar allí la siesta,
a beber en el Tajo mi ganado;
y después de llegado,
sin saber de cuál arte,

Ah, flow, my tears, stream forth without remorse.
    Because of you, the dim and silent forest,
because of you, the lonely and remote
solitary places did always please me;
because of you green grass, the cool, fresh wind,
pure white lilies, roses of crimson red,
and beautiful sweet spring were my desire.
Ah, how I was deceived!
Ah, how different it was,
how contrary and distinct
all that lay hidden in your lying heart!
How clear the voice of the sinister crow
telling me, repeating over again
the truth of my misfortune.
Ah, flow, my tears, stream forth without remorse.
    How often, as I slept in the wild places,
though it appeared so senseless, a mere whim,
did I, ah woe, see my own grief in dreams!
I dreamed it was summer, that I was leading
my flock to the gold banks of the river Tagus[5]
there to drink and rest in the midday heat;
and then, when I arrived,
not knowing how or why,

[5]The Tajo, or Tagus, River, which runs through Spain and Portugal, was fabled
to have sands of gold along its banks.

por desusada parte
y por nuevo camino el agua se iba;
ardiendo yo con la calor estiva,
el curso enajenado iba siguiendo
del agua fugitiva.
Salid sin duelo, lágrimas, corriendo.

    Tu dulce habla ¿en cúya oreja suena?
Tus claros ojos ¿a quién los volviste?
¿Por quién tan sin respeto me trocaste?
Tu quebrantada fe ¿dó la pusiste?
¿Cuál es el cuello que, como en cadena,
de tus hermosos brazos anudaste?
No hay corazón que baste,
aunque fuese de piedra,
viendo mi amada hiedra,
de mí arrancada, en otro muro asida,
y mi parra en otro olmo entretejida,
que no se esté con llanto deshaciendo
hasta acabar la vida.
Salid sin duelo, lágrimas, corriendo.

    ¿Qué no se esperará de aquí adelante,
por difícil que sea y por incierto?
O ¿qué discordia no será juntada?,
y juntamente ¿qué tendrá por cierto,
o qué de hoy más no temerá el amante,
siendo a todo materia por ti dada?

I saw the water change its course
and flow where it had never flowed before;
and I, caught in the burning heat of summer,
kept following the unexpected path
of the fugitive river.
Ah, flow, my tears, stream forth without remorse.
 Your sweet speech, in whose ear does it now sound?
Your clear, bright eyes, to whom have you now turned them?
With whom have you replaced me, faithless one?
The promises you broke, where did you hide them?
Whose neck did you bind in your lovely arms
as if entwining it in heavy chains?
No heart is hard enough,
even if made of stone,
to see my beloved ivy
torn from me to cling fast to another wall,
my grapevine turning round another elm,
and not break down and be undone by weeping
till life comes to an end.
Ah, flow, my tears, stream forth without remorse.
 What cannot befall us now, from this day on,
no matter how unlikely or how harsh?
What discord or what strife will not prevail?
Then too, what will the lover hold as certain
from now on, what will the lover not fear
since you have given any act a cause?

Cuando tú enajenada
de mi cuidado fuiste,
notable causa diste,
y ejemplo a todos cuantos cubre el cielo,
que el más seguro tema con recelo
perder lo que estuviere poseyendo.
Salid fuera sin duelo,
salid sin duelo, lágrimas, corriendo.

    Materia diste al mundo de esperanza
de alcanzar lo imposible y no pensado,
y de hacer juntar lo diferente,
dando a quien diste el corazón malvado,
quitándolo de mí con tal mudanza
que siempre sonará de gente en gente.
La cordera paciente
con el lobo hambriento
hará su ayuntamiento,
y con las simples aves sin ruido
harán las bravas sierpes ya su nido;
que mayor diferencia comprehendo
de ti al que has escogido.
Salid sin duelo, lágrimas, corriendo.

    Siempre de nueva leche en el verano
v en el invierno abundo; en mi majada
la manteca y el queso está sobrado;
de mi cantar, pues, yo te vi agradada

Oh, when you left, forsaking
me and my love for you,
you gave the clearest reason,
an example to all men 'neath the sun,
why the most certain man should learn to doubt,
should fear the loss of all he may possess.
Ah, flow without remorse,
ah, flow, my tears, stream forth without remorse.

   You gave to the world every reason to hope
it might achieve th'unthought of, th'impossible,
uniting opposites and making them one,
when you gave your untrue heart to another,
took it from me in a change so unforeseen
that it will always be a reason for talk.
The patient, gentle lamb
will join and lie down next to
the hungry, ravening wolf,
and with the simple, noiseless birds of air
ferocious serpents now will make their nests;
for I see greater differences between
you and your chosen one.
Ah, flow, my tears, stream forth without remorse.

   In hottest summer I always have fresh milk;
and in frozen winter, there in the fold,
abundant stores of cheese and of sweet butter;
and my singing, I saw it pleased you so

tanto que no pudiera el mantuano
Títiro ser de ti más alabado.
No soy, pues, bien mirado,
tan disforme ni feo;
que aun agora me veo
en esta agua que corre clara y pura,
y cierto no trocara mi figura
con ese que de mí se está riendo;
¡trocara mi ventura!
Salid sin duelo, lágrimas, corriendo.

   ¿Cómo te vine en tanto menosprecio?
¿Cómo te fuí tan presto aborrecible?
¿Cómo te faltó en mí el conocimiento?
Si no tuvieras condición terrible,
siempre fuera tenido de ti en precio,
y no viera de ti este apartamiento.
¿No sabes que sin cuento
buscan en el estío
mis ovejas el frío
de la sierra de Cuenca, y el gobierno
del abrigado Estremo en el invierno?

that even Virgil's Mantuan Tityrus[6]
could not be more lauded and praised by you.
Consider this: I am not
so ugly or deformed;
even now I see my face
in this pure water flowing limpid, clear,
and truth is I would not exchange my face
with that mocking man who laughs at me now,
but I would exchange my fate!
Ah, flow, my tears, stream forth without remorse.

   How did I come to be so scorned by you?
How did you find me loathsome and base so soon?
How did your good opinion of me vanish?
If you were not in this vile, dreadful state,
I would always and still have your esteem,
I would not see you turn away from me.
You must know that in summer
large numbers of my sheep
seek out the cooler air
of the Cuenca mountains, and then in winter
the shelter of a warmer Extremadura.[7]

---

[6]Tityrus was the principal shepherd in Virgil's first eclogue, and is tradition-
ally associated with the Mantuan poet—that is, Virgil.

[7]Cuenca and Extremadura are Spanish provinces: Cuenca is located in the cen-
ter of the country, and Extremadura is in the west, along the Portuguese border.

Mas ¡qué vale el tener, si derritiendo
me estoy en llanto eterno!
Salid sin duelo, lágrimas, corriendo.

    Con mi llorar las piedras enternecen
su natural dureza y la quebrantan;
los árboles parece que se inclinan:
las aves que me escuchan, cuando cantan,
con diferente voz se condolecen,
y mi morir cantando me adivinan;
las fieras, que reclinan
su cuerpo fatigado,
dejan el sosegado
sueño por escuchar mi llanto triste:
tú sola contra mí te endureciste,
los ojos aun siquiera no volviendo
a lo que tú heciste.
Salid sin duelo, lágrimas, corriendo.

    Mas ya que a socorrer aquí no vienes,
no dejes el lugar que tanto amaste,
que bien podrás venir de mí segura.
Yo dejaré el lugar do me dejaste;
ven, si por solo esto te detienes.
Ves aquí un prado lleno de verdura,
ves aquí una espesura,
ves aquí una agua clara,
en otro tiempo cara,

But what use are possessions when I dissolve
in endless tears and weeping!
Ah, flow, my tears, stream forth without remorse.

    With my weeping, the very stones do soften
their natural hardness and then break apart;
the trees appear to bend, leaning toward the earth:
the birds that listen to me, when they sing,
with different voices mourn with me and grieve
and they foretell my death in every song;
the wild beasts that lie down
to rest their weary bodies
abandon peaceful sleep
to listen to the sad sound of my weeping:
you alone have hardened your heart against me,
not even turning your eyes toward me to see,
alas, what you have done.
Ah, flow, my tears, stream forth without remorse.

    But though you do not come here to console me,
do not abandon the place you loved so well,
for you can come here and be safe from me.
I shall leave this place, the place where you forsook me;
come, if that is all that hinders you.
Here you see a meadow, a field of green,
and here a thicket, and hedges,
and here the crystal water,
once, in times past, so dear

a quien de ti con lágrimas me quejo.
Quizá aquí hallarás, pues yo me alejo,
al que todo mi bien quitarme puede;
que pues el bien le dejo,
no es mucho que el lugar también le quede.—
    Aquí dió fin a su cantar Salicio,
y sospirando en el postrero acento,
soltó de llanto una profunda vena.
Queriendo el monte al grave sentimiento
de aquel dolor en algo ser propicio,
con la pesada voz retumba y suena.
La blanca Filomena,
casi como dolida
y a compasión movida,
dulcemente responde al són lloroso.
Lo que cantó tras esto Nemoroso
decildo vos Piérides, que tanto
no puedo yo ni oso,
que siento enflaquecer mi débil canto.

where now I shed my tears lamenting you.
Here you will find, may be, for I am leaving,
the one who has taken all my happiness;
if I leave my every joy,
what matter if he also keeps the place?"

    Here Salicio brought to an end his song,
and sighing as he sang the final word,
he opened a deep vein of anguished tears.
The mountain, wishing in some way to support
his somber feelings of sorrow and of grief
resounds and echoes with its heavy voice.
And fair white Philomena,[8]
as if in mourning too
and moved to feel compassion,
responds so sweetly to the tearful plaint.
What was sung after this by Nemoroso,
O Muses, you must say, for I cannot
and dare not attempt so much:
I feel my feeble song grow ever weaker.

[8]There are several versions of the Greek myth, later adapted by Ovid. The victim, called either Philomela or Philomena, was assaulted by Tereus, identified either as her husband or her brother-in-law. To hide his crime, Tereus cut out her tongue; depending on the version of the story, she was turned into a nightingale or a swallow by the gods.

Nemoroso

   Corrientes aguas, puras, cristalinas,
árboles que os estáis mirando en ellas,
verde prado de fresca sombra lleno,
aves que aquí sembrás vuestras querellas,
hiedra que por los árboles caminas
torciendo el paso por su verde seno:
yo me vi tan ajeno
del grave mal que siento,
que de puro contento
con vuestra soledad me recreaba,
donde con dulce sueño reposaba,
o con el pensamiento discurría
por donde no hallaba
sino memorias llenas de alegría.

   Y en este mismo valle, donde agora
me entristezco y me canso en el reposo,
estuve ya contento y descansado.
¡Oh bien caduco, vano y presuroso!
Acuérdome, durmiendo aquí algún hora,
que despertando, a Elisa vi a mi lado.
¡Oh miserable hado!
¡Oh tela delicada,

Nemoroso

   O flowing waters, so pure and crystalline,
and trees that see yourselves reflected there,
and you, green meadow, filled with cooling shade,
birds that sow here your plaints and lamentations,
ivy that wanders up the mighty trees,
winding your way along their green-hued bosoms:
I saw myself so removed
from the anguish I feel now
that in my pure contentment
I took pleasure in your silent solitude,
where I would rest in sweet and tranquil slumber
or visit again in my thoughts those places
where I found only joy and
memories overflowing with sheer gladness.

   And in this very same valley where I now
am saddened and can find no rest in sleep,
I once was contented, filled with repose.
O passing joy, so fleeting and so frail!
Once, I recall, when I was sleeping here
I woke to find Elisa[9] at my side.
O wretched, awful fate!
O delicate fine cloth

[9]A name traditionally associated with the pastoral tradition.

antes de tiempo dada
a los agudos filos de la muerte!,
más convenible suerte
a los cansados años de mi vida,
que es más que el hierro fuerte,
pues no la ha quebrantado tu partida.

 ¿Dó están agora aquellos claros ojos
que llevaban tras sí, como colgada,
mi alma doquier que ellos se volvían?
¿Dó está la blanca mano delicada,
llena de vencimientos y despojos
que de mí mis sentidos le ofrecían?
Los cabellos que vían
con gran desprecio el oro,
como a menor tesoro,
¿adónde están? ¿Adónde el blando pecho?
¿Dó la coluna que el dorado techo
con presunción graciosa sostenía?
Aquesto todo agora ya se encierra,
por desventura mía,
en la fría, desierta y dura tierra.

 ¿Quién me dijera, Elisa, vida mía,

subjected before its time
to the sharp, cutting blades wielded by Death!
an end much better suited
to the slow, weary years of this sad life,
stronger and more enduring than hard steel,
for it has not been shattered by your leaving.

    Where are they now, those clear and limpid eyes
that took with them, as if it were attached,
my soul, no matter where those eyes might turn?
Where now is the delicate, pale white hand
that held conquest of me and all the spoils
that my bedazzled senses offered her?
The hair that looked with scorn
on precious, shining gold
as a lesser treasure,
where is it now? And where that gentle bosom?
And the long, slender column
that held the golden dome high
with so much pride and grace?
All of it, all is now enclosed, contained,
to my eternal woe,
in the cold and hard, the desolate earth.

    Who could have told me, Elisa, my life,

cuando en aqueste valle al fresco viento
andábamos cogiendo tiernas flores,
que habíe de ver con largo apartamiento
venir el triste y solitario día
que diese amargo fin a mis amores?
El cielo en mis dolores
cargó la mano tanto
que a sempiterno llanto
y a triste soledad me ha condenado;
y lo que siento más es verme atado
a la pesada vida y enojosa,
solo, desamparado,
ciego, sin lumbre, en cárcel tenebrosa.

    Despúes que nos dejaste, nunca pace
en hartura el ganado ya, ni acude
el campo al labrador con mano llena.
No hay bien que en mal no se convierta y mude:
la mala hierba al trigo ahoga, y nace
en lugar suyo la infelice avena;
la tierra, que de buena
gana nos producía
flores con que solía
quitar en sólo vellas mil enojos,
produce agora en cambio estos abrojos,
ya de rigor de espinas intratable;
yo hago con mis ojos

when in this valley, in its fresh, cool breezes,
you and I roamed and picked its tender blossoms,
that I would have to see this endless absence,
the dreadful day, mournful and solitary,
that put so dire an end to all my love?
Heaven has filled its hand
with so much grief for me, and so much sorrow,
that I have been condemned
to endless tears and grievous solitude;
what I regret the most is being bound
to life grown burdensome and full of woe,
I am alone and helpless,
blind and without light in a darkened cell.

    Since you left us, the cattle never more
have grazed their fill, nor does the field now offer
with open hand its bounty to the farmer.
There is no good that does not change to evil:
the weed strangles the wheat, and in its place
a wretched crop of oats is born and thrives;
the earth was willing once
to bring forth flowers for us
—the sight of them took away
a thousand cares and woes, a thousand griefs—
but now the earth gives only thistles and tares,
so many thorns that it cannot be tilled;
with my eyes raining tears,

crecer, lloviendo, el fruto miserable.

    Como al partir del sol la sombra crece,
y en cayendo su rayo se levanta
la negra escuridad que el mundo cubre,
de do viene el temor que nos espanta
y la medrosa forma en que se ofrece
aquella que la noche nos encubre,
hasta que el sol descubre
su luz pura y hermosa:
tal es la tenebrosa
noche de tu partir, en que he quedado
de sombra y de temor atormentado,
hasta que muerte el tiempo determine
que a ver el deseado
sol de tu clara vista me encamine.

    Cual suele el ruiseñor con triste canto
quejarse, entre las hojas escondido,
del duro labrador, que cautamente
le despojó su caro y dulce nido
de los tiernos hijuelos entre tanto
que del amado ramo estaba ausente,
y aquel dolor que siente
con diferencia tanta
por la dulce garganta
despide, y a su canto el aire suena,
y la callada noche no refrena

I water this bitter fruit and make it grow.
    As the sun departs, the shadows mount,
and when its light sets, then the ebon dark,
the blackness rises, spreads, envelops the world,
the source of the terror that frightens us,
and of the fearsome forms taken and assumed
by those things that the night conceals from us,
until the sun shows once more
its pure and beautiful light:
this is like the nocturnal
shadows that your departure has left to me,
tormented by the darkness and by fear
until death will select and choose the time
to lead me to the vision
of my long-desired sun: the sight of you.
    As the nightingale with a mournful song
complains, hidden among the leaves, lamenting
the merciless farmer, who with heartless stealth
robbed the nest of all her tender fledglings
while she was absent from the well-loved branch,
and the pain of the nightingale
fills her throat, turns to melody
utterly altered and changed,
and the night remains silent and does not restrain
her devoted lamentations and complaints,
and brings heaven and the stars

su lamentable oficio y sus querellas,
trayendo de su pena
al cielo por testigo y las estrellas:
    desta manera suelto ya la rienda
a mi dolor, y así me quejo en vano
de la dureza de la muerte airada;
ella en mi corazón metió la mano
y de allí me llevó mi dulce prenda,
que aqué era su nido y su morada.
Ay muerte arrebatada!
Por ti me estoy quejando
al cielo y enojando
con importuno llanto al mundo todo:
el desigual dolor no sufre modo.
No me podrán quitar el dolorido
sentir, si ya del todo
primero no me quitan el sentido.
    Tengo una parte aquí de tus cabellos,
Elisa, envueltos en un blanco paño,
que nunca de mi seno se me apartan;
descójolos, y de un dolor tamaño
enternecerme siento que sobre ellos
nunca mis ojos de llorar se hartan.
Sin que de allí se partan,
con sospiros calientes,
más que la llama ardientes,

to bear witness to her terrible grief:
    in this same manner I now give free rein
to my sorrow, and I lament in vain
the harsh ire, the pitiless wrath of Death,
who thrust a cruel hand deep into my heart
where she did find and steal my dearest love,
for there love had her nest and her abode.
O Death so full of fury!
Because of you I weep and cry
to Heaven; I am wearisome
to th'entire world with ceaseless tears:
my overflowing grief allows no check.
No one can ever take away from me
this woe or sense of loss unless
he takes away from me all other feeling.
    Here I keep a lock of your lovely hair,
Elisa, enclosed in a pure-white cloth:
never is it parted from my bosom;
I gaze upon your tresses and dissolve
in grief so vast I feel that my poor eyes
never will tire of weeping over them.
I do not move them away,
and with ardent sighs that burn
hotter than fire or flame,

los enjugo del llanto, y de consuno
casi los paso y cuento uno a uno;
juntándolos, con un cordon los ato.
Tras esto el importuno
dolor me deja descansar un rato.
    Mas luego a la memoria se me ofrece
aquella noche tenebrosa, escura,
que tanto aflige esta anima mezquina
con la memoria de mi desventura.
Verte presente agora me parece
en aquel duro trance de Lucina;
y aquella voz divina,
con cuyo son y acentos
a los airados vientos
pudieras amansar, que agora es muda,
me parece que oigo, que a la cruda,
inesorable diosa demandabas
en aquel paso ayuda;
y tú, rústica diosa, ¿dónde estabas?
    ¿Íbate tanto en perseguir las fieras?
¿Íbate tanto en un pastor dormido?

I dry the lock of hair, wiping my tears,
and almost count one by one each strand of hair;
with ribbon I tie them together again.
Then my unending woe
relents for a brief moment and lets me rest.
      But oh, the persistent memory of that
dark night of shadows returns, and so afflicts
my wretched spirit with dire memories
of my misfortune that I must grieve again.
Now I seem to see you present, suffering
through the crisis, Lucina's[10] cruel birth pangs;
and the divine voice that is yours,
those accents and that tone
that you could have used to calm
fierce and furious winds, that voice now mute—
I seem to hear it as you called upon
the goddess, harsh and inexorable, for help
in that dark and dreadful moment;
and you, rustic goddess, where were you then?
      Were you so caught up in pursuing beasts?
Were you so caught up in a slumbering shepherd?[11]

[10]The Roman goddess of birth, she was an aspect of Juno and is associated here with Diana, goddess of the hunt and of the moon.

[11]In Greek mythology, Endymion was loved by several goddesses, who descended from heaven to watch him as he slept.

¿Cosa pudo bastar a tal crueza,
que, conmovida a compasión, oído
a los votos y lágrimas no dieras
por no ver hecha tierra tal belleza,
o no ver la tristeza
en que tu Nemoroso
queda, que su reposo
era seguir tu oficio, persiguiendo
las fieras por los montes, y ofreciendo
a tus sagradas aras los despojos?
¿Y tú, ingrata, riendo,
dejas morir mi bien ante los ojos?

   Divina Elisa, pues agora el cielo
con inmortales pies pisas y mides,
y su mudanza ves, estando queda,
¿por qué de mí te olvidas y no pides
que se apresure el tiempo en que este velo
rompa del cuerpo, y verme libre pueda,
y en la tercera rueda
contigo mano a mano
busquemos otro llano,
busquemos otros montes y otros ríos,
otros valles floridos y sombríos,

What could be just cause for so much cruelty
that, moved to compassion, you gave no ear
to the vows she swore, the tears she shed, so you
would not see her beauty turned to mere earth,
and would not see the sadness
in which your Nemoroso
is left, for his delight
was to follow your lead, pursuing beasts
through the wild mountains and then to offer
them to you upon your sacred altars?
Yet you, ungrateful, laughing,
allow my love to die before your eyes?
    Divine Elisa, who with immortal feet
now wander and roam and measure heaven
and see all its changes, when you are still,
oh why do you forget me and not ask
that the time be hastened when I can sunder
the veil of this body, at last be free,
and then in the third circle[12]
search with you, hand in hand,
search for another meadow,
search for other mountains and other rivers,
other flowering valleys full of shade,

[12]In Ptolemaic cosmology, the third circle is the sphere of Venus as it circles
the earth.

donde descanse y siempre pueda verte
ante los ojos míos,
sin miedo y sobresalto de perderte?—
    Nunca pusieran fin al triste lloro
los pastores, ni fueran acabadas
las canciones que solo el monte oía,
si mirando las nubes coloradas,
al tramontar del sol bordadas de oro,
no vieran que era ya pasado el día.
La sombra se veía
venir corriendo apriesa
ya por la falda espesa
del altísimo monte, y recordando
ambos como de sueño, y acabando
el fugitivo sol, de luz escaso,
su ganado llevando,
se fueron recogiendo paso a paso.

where I can rest, where I can see you always
before these eyes of mine,
free of fear, the great blow of losing you?—
    Never would the shepherds have put an end
to their laments, or their sweet, mournful songs,
heard only by mountains untamed and desolate,
have ceased, if, looking at crimson-hued clouds
embroidered in gold by the setting sun,
they had not seen the close of day upon them.
The shadows came descending,
moving apace, hastening
down the overgrown slope
of the loftiest mountain, and the two,
as if waking from a dream, and in
the scant light of the sun
in flight, and then gone,
brought together their sheep
and slowly, step by step, the shepherds left.

Fray Luis de León

(1527–1591)

L uis de León was born in Belmonte, Cuenca, to a family of *conversos*, or Jews forced to convert to Christianity. He studied at the University of Salamanca and later became an Augustinian friar (*Fray* is his religious title). A professor of scriptural studies at Salamanca, he made a good number of enemies among the faculty and especially among members of the Dominican Order, not only because of his *converso* background but because he insisted on the importance of Hebrew in the text of the Old Testament (as opposed to the Vulgate translations into Latin). As a result of these conflicts, he was denounced to the Inquisition and spent the next four years in prison until he was finally acquitted. Legend has it that when he returned to the university, he began his first class with the words, "As I was saying the other day . . ." He edited the works of Saint Teresa of Ávila—the mystic, the reformer of the Carmelites, and the mentor of Saint John of the Cross. Shortly before his death, Fray Luis was elected provincial of the Augustinians.

Fray Luis wrote scholarly works in Latin; he also composed more popular works for the faithful in Spanish and produced translations of biblical works (the Book of Job, the Song of Solomon, and selections from the Psalms and Proverbs) and of Latin poetry, particularly works by Virgil and Horace, whose writings had a significant influence on his own. Almost all of his twenty-six original poems are written in the "lyre" stanza originated by Garcilaso (see p. 39).

Fray Luis is generally considered a leading poet in the far-reaching "Christianization" of the Renaissance in Spain during the sixteenth century. This meant that as a consequence of the Counter-Reformation, and especially of the judgments and rulings of the Council of Trent (1545–1563), the secular Italianate forms and themes brought into Spain by Garcilaso were used by subsequent writers to explore moral, spiritual, and religious topics. The poets and humanists who were the followers of Fray Luis in the sixteenth century formed the influential "School of Salamanca."

His poetry remained in manuscript until it was finally published in 1631 by Francisco de Quevedo (see p. 169), an ardent admirer of his writing.

Décima

Aqui la envidia y mentira
me tuvieron encerrado.
Dichoso el humilde estado
del sabio que se retira
de aqueste mundo malvado,
y con pobre mesa y casa,
en el campo deleitoso
con sólo Dios se compasa,
y a solas su vida pasa,
ni envidiado ni envidioso.

Stanza

Upon Leaving Prison

    Here is where envy and lies
had me imprisoned for years.
Oh happy the humble state
of the man wise enough to flee
the spite of this venom'd world,
and with humble hearth and home
in the pleasant countryside,
and God as his sole companion,
he shuns the presence of men,
not envious, and envied by none.

Oda III

A Francisco Salinas
Catedrático de Música de la
Universidad de Salamanca

El aire se serena
y viste de hermosura y luz no usada,
Salinas, cuando suena
la música extremada,
por vuestra sabia mano gobernada;
    a cuyo son divino
mi alma, que en olvido está sumida,
torna a cobrar el tino
y memoria perdida
de su origen primera esclarecida.
    Y como se conoce,
en suerte y pensamientos se mejora;
el oro desconoce,
que el vulgo ciego adora,
la belleza caduca, engañadora.
    Traspasa el aire todo
hasta llegar a la más alta esfera,
y oye allí otro modo

Ode III

To Francisco Salinas
Professor of Music at the
University of Salamanca

The air becomes calm, serene,
and dons a rare beauty, an unknown light,
O Salinas, every time
magnificent music sounds,
guided and led by your deft, learned hand;
    at that glorious sound divine
my soul, mired deep in all it has forgotten
regains its bearings and course,
the memory that was lost
of origins and its first, noble home.[1]
    And as it learns what it is
my soul mends its fate, purifies its thoughts,
and turns away from the gold
adored by the sightless mob,
the transient deceit that they call fair.
    It ascends, piercing the air,
climbing till it reaches the highest sphere,[2]
where it hears another mode,

[1] The poet alludes to the traditional concept that the soul leaves Heaven in order to be born into a body, forgetting its divine nature during its time on earth.

[2] In the Pythagorean vision of the universe, the divine realm was fixed, while circling around it were the planets and other heavenly bodies, each in its own sphere. Their musically and mathematically harmonious relationship to one another created what was known as "the music of the spheres."

de no perecedera
música, que es de todas la primera.

    Ve cómo el gran maestro,
a aquesta inmensa cítara aplicado,
con movimiento diestro
produce el son sagrado,
con que este eterno templo es sustentado.

    Y como está compuesta
de números concordes, luego envía
consonante respuesta;
y entrambas a porfía
mezclan una dulcísima armonía.

    Aquí la alma navega
por un mar de dulzura, y finalmente
en él ansí se anega
que ningún accidente
extraño y peregrino oye o siente.

    ¡Oh, desmayo dichoso!
¡Oh, muerte que das vida! ¡Oh, dulce olvido!
¡Durase en tu reposo,

the music that never dies,
the origin and source of all the rest.

   It sees the Musician divine[3]
playing on the strings of His vast harp,
and with a great dextrous hand
creating the sacred sound
that for the eternal temple[4] is support.

   And because it is composed
of concordant numbers, it then sends forth
its own musical response;
the sounds contend and combine,
creating the sweetest of all harmonies.

   And now the soul sails, it floats
in a sea of sweet bliss, and then at last
it sinks and drowns in the sea
and does not sense or hear
any accidental sound, foreign or strange.

   O blessed, fortunate swoon!
O death that gives me life, O sweetest loss![5]
If I could but stay in you,

---

[3]The creator. Here music is equivalent to the creative Logos.

[4]The reference is to Heaven.

[5]Here, and in the preceding stanza, the poet evokes the ecstasy of his approach to God, where the soul's life is most intense. This is the near-mystical effect of Salinas's music.

sin ser restituído
jamás a aqueste bajo y vil sentido!
    A aqueste bien os llamo,
gloria del apolíneo sacro coro,
amigos a quien amo
sobre todo tesoro;
que todo lo demás es triste lloro.
    ¡Oh! suene de contino,
Salinas, vuestro son en mis oídos,
por quien al bien divino
despiertan los sentidos,
quedando a lo demás amortecidos.

and never again return
to this base world of senses coarse and vile!
   To this joy I call you all,
glory of Apollo's sacred choir,[6]
O good friends whom I love more
than any wealth or treasure;
the rest is nothing more than anguished tears.
   Let your music always sound,
Salinas, echoing sweet in my ears,
it lets my senses awake
to divine joy and delight
and makes them deaf to any lesser thing.

[6]Apollo, originally the Greek god of shepherds, was also the god of all the arts, including music. By association, the poet alludes to Christ the Good Shepherd and to the joys of rustic life.

Oda VIII

Cuando contemplo el cielo
de innumerables luces adornado,
y miro hacia el suelo,
de noche rodeado,
en sueño y en olvido sepultado,
    el amor y la pena
despiertan en mi pecho un ansia ardiente;
despiden larga vena
los ojos hechos fuente;
la lengua dice al fin con voz doliente:
    «Morada de grandeza,
templo de claridad y hermosura:
mi alma que a tu alteza
nació, ¿qué desventura
la tiene en esta cárcel baja, escura?
    »¿Qué mortal desatino
de la verdad aleja ansí el sentido,
que de tu bien divino
olvidado, perdido,
sigue la vana sombra, el bien fingido?
    »El hombre está entregado
al sueño, de su suerte no cuidando;
y con paso callado

Ode VIII
Quiet Night

    When I contemplate the heavens
embellished and adorned with countless lights,
then look down at the earth
enveloped in dark night
and buried deep in oblivion and sleep,
    the love and sorrow I feel
awaken in my breast an ardent longing;
my eyes, become like fountains,
let flow abundant streams,
and at last, in woeful tones, my voice does call:
    "Oh, home of so much grandeur,
temple of light, of clarity, of beauty:
my soul was born for your heights,
yet what immense misfortune
keeps it in this vile prison, in the dark?
    "What mortal misperception
moves my senses so far away from truth
that, leaving your sacred good,
forgetting they wander, lost,
following vain shadows, illusions of good?
    "Man is given over
wholly to sleep, not caring for his fate,
while heaven, with silent steps,

el cielo, vueltas dando,
las horas del vivir le va hurtando.
    »¡Ay!, despertad, mortales!
Mirad con atención en vuestro daño.
¿Las almas inmortales,
hechas a bien tamaño,
podrán vivir de sombra y solo engaño?
    »¡Ay!, levantad los ojos
a aquesta celestial eterna esfera:
burlaréis los antojos
de aquesa lisonjera
vida, con cuanto teme y cuanto espera.
    »¿Es más que un breve punto
el bajo y torpe suelo, comparado
a aqueste gran trasunto,
do vive mejorado
lo que es, lo que será, lo que ha pasado?
    »Quien mira el gran concierto
de aquestos resplandores eternales,
su movimiento cierto,
sus pasos desiguales
y en proporción concorde tan iguales:
    »la luna cómo mueve
la plateada rueda, y va en pos de ella

keeps turning round, keeps turning,
stealing from him the hours of his life.
   "Oh, mortal men, awake!
Open your eyes and see the harm you do.
Can your immortal souls,
created for such great good,
survive on shadows and on mere deceit?
   "Oh, lift up your eyes and look
at the everlasting sphere celestial:
you will see through th'illusions
of this alluring life,
and all it fears and all it must desire.
   "Is this base and torpid earth
more than a tiny speck when we compare it
to that great transfigured place
where in a heightened state
dwells what is, what will be, and what has been?
   "Whoever looks upon
this great harmony of eternal lights,[1]
their movement certain and sure,
their steps so unalike,
yet the same in proportion and consonance,
   "he sees how the moon does move
its silvery sphere, and behind her comes

---

[1]The reference is to the heavens and the movement of the spheres.

la luz do el saber llueve,
y la graciosa estrella
de Amor la sigue reluciente y bella;
    »y cómo otro camino
prosigue el sanguinoso Marte airado,
y el Júpiter benino,
de bienes mil cercado,
serena el cielo con su rayo amado;
    »rodéase en la cumbre
Saturno, padre de los siglos de oro;
tras dél la muchedumbre
del reluciente coro
su luz va repartiendo y su tesoro:
    »¿quién es el que esto mira
y precia la bajeza de la tierra,
y no gime y suspira
por romper lo que encierra
el alma y de estos bienes la destierra?
    »Aquí vive el contento,
aquí reina la paz; aquí, asentado
en rico y alto asiento,
está el Amor sagrado,
de glorias y deleites rodeado.
    »Inmensa hermosura
aquí se muestra toda, y resplandece

the light where wisdom pours down,
and then the star of grace
the brilliant star of Love follows in beauty;
     "and how another path
is taken by Mars, wrathful and blood-stained,
and Jupiter the benign,
amid blessings past number,
calms the heavens with his beloved light;
     "and at their heights is circling
Saturn, father of all the golden ages;
behind him comes a throng,
a brilliant, shining choir
dispensing his light and treasure to ev'ryone:
     "who can gaze upon these spheres
and value the dark lowliness of earth,
and not weep and groan and sigh
to shatter what imprisons
his soul and keeps it distant from these blessings?
     "Here dwells true contentment,
here tranquility reigns; here,
on a rich and lofty seat
sits holy Love divine,
encircled by all glories and delights.
     "A divine beauty is here
fully revealed, and here it shines in brilliance—

clarísima luz pura,
que jamás anochece;
eterna primavera aquí florece.
    »¡Oh, campos verdaderos!
¡Oh, prados con verdad dulces y amenos!
¡Riquísimos mineros!
¡Oh, deleitosos senos!
¡Repuestos valles, de mil bienes llenos!»

the purest, clearest light
that never dims to night,
and an eternal springtime blossoms here.
    "O fields forever true!
O meadows sweet and pleasant with the truth!
O lodes and seams rich with ore!
O hollows filled with delight!
Secluded vales that hold a thousand blessings!"

Oda XIX

¡Y dejas, Pastor santo,
tu grey en este valle hondo, escuro,
con soledad y llanto!
Y tú rompiendo el puro
aire, ¿te vas al inmortal seguro?

　　Los antes bienhadados,
y los agora tristes y afligidos,
a tus pechos criados,
de ti desposeídos,
¿a dó convertirán ya sus sentidos?

　　¿Qué mirarán los ojos
que vieron de tu rostro la hermosura,
que no les sea enojos?
Quien oyó tu dulzura,
¿qué no tendrá por sordo y desventura?

　　Aqueste mar turbado,
¿quién le pondrá ya freno? ¿Quién concierto
al viento fiero, airado?
Estando tú encubierto,
¿qué norte guiará la nave al puerto?

Ode XIX

ON THE ASCENSION

You're leaving, holy Shepherd,[1]
your flock here in this valley deep and dark,
and they, alone and weeping,
while you, ever ascending,
are you bound for your immortal citadel?
  And those who once knew contentment
but now are filled with grieving and deep sorrow,
nurtured in Your fair bosom
and then by You dispossessed,
where can they turn their senses so deprived?
  What can those eyes look upon,
once having seen the beauty of Your face,
that will not seem base and foul?
To those who heard Your sweet voice,
what sound will not seem dissonant and flat?
  This rough and tumultuous sea,
who now will hold it back? And who will calm
the fiercely raging wind?
When You are hidden from view,
what Star will guide our fragile ship to port?

[1]The Shepherd is Jesus, addressed by His flock of followers as He ascends to heaven.

¡Ay!, nube, envidïosa
aun de este breve gozo, ¿qué te aquejas?
¿Dó vuelas presurosa?
¡Cuán rica tú te alejas!
¡Cuán pobres y cuán ciegos, ay, nos dejas!

Oh woe, oh cloud[2] so envious
still of our brief joy, what spurs you on?
Where do you hasten and fly?
What wealth is yours departing,
alas, how poor you leave us, and how blind!

[2]Jesus is traditionally depicted as ascending to Heaven on a cloud.

SAN JUAN DE LA CRUZ

(1542–1591)

Widely known in English as Saint John of the Cross, the poet was born Juan de Yepes, in humble circumstances. He studied at the University of Salamanca and became a disciple of Saint Teresa of Ávila in the bitterly fought effort to reform the Spanish Carmelites. Eventually he was placed in a harsh conventual prison in Toledo by his dissident, unreformed Carmelite brothers. This, apparently, is where he composed the *Cántico espiritual*, or Spiritual Canticle, without benefit of writing implements, depending solely on his memory. The last years of his life were much less turbulent. He spent them in near-isolation, which he desired, in Andalusia. He died in Ubeda, in the Spanish province of Jaén.

One of the great European mystics and an exceptional poet, San Juan is best known for three relatively brief poems, inspired by the biblical Song of Songs, or Song of Solomon, and written exclusively in Garcilaso's "lyre" stanza form (see p. 39), which was also used by Fray Luis de León. These three poems—"Noche oscura del alma" [Dark Night of the Soul], "Cántico espiritual" [Spiritual Canticle], and "Llama de amor viva" [Flame of Living Love]— accompanied by four long prose treatises that explicate the theological significance of each line, are informed by a rapturously erotic imagery that goes far beyond traditional approaches to religion in its expression of the ecstatic ineffability of the soul's union with God.

San Juan was beatified in 1675, canonized in 1726, and declared a Doctor of the Church in 1926. His writings were deemed by the Roman Catholic Church to be as authoritative in mystical knowledge as Saint Thomas Aquinas's are in theology.

Canción II: La Noche Oscura

Canciones

De el alma que se goza de haber llegado
al alto estado de la perfección, que
es la unión con Dios, por el camino
de la negación espiritual.

1. En una noche oscura,
con ansias en amores inflamada,
¡oh dichosa ventura!,
salí sin ser notada,
estando ya mi casa sosegada:

2. a escuras y segura,
por la secreta escala disfrazada,
¡oh dichosa ventura!,
a escuras y en celada,
estando ya mi casa sosegada;

3. en la noche dichosa,
en secreto, que nadie me veía,
ni yo miraba cosa,
sin otra luz y guía
sino la que en el corazón ardía.

4. Aquésta me guïaba
más cierto que la luz del mediodía,
a donde me esperaba
quien yo bien me sabía,
en parte donde nadie parecía.

Song II: The Dark Night

Songs
Of the soul that rejoices at having reached
the high state of perfection, which
is union with God, by means of the path
of spiritual denial of the self

1. On a dark night, deep and black,
when I, on fire with the passions of love
—what great good fortune was mine!—
slipped out, hidden, unseen,
when my sleeping house was silent and still;

2. and protected in the dark,
concealed by the quiet, secret staircase
—what great good fortune was mine!—
in the ebon dark, well-hidden
when my sleeping house was silent and still;

3. and on that fortunate night,
in secret, when no one's eyes could see me,
I saw nothing around me
and had no light or guide
but the one that was blazing in my heart.

4. This was the fire that led me,
more clear and certain than the light of noon,
to where he waited for me
—I knew who he was, oh I knew—
there where no one was seen, no one appeared.

5. ¡Oh noche que guiaste!,
¡oh noche amable más que el alborada!,
¡oh noche que juntaste
amado con amada,
amada en el amado transformada!

6. En mi pecho florido,
que entero para él solo se guardaba,
allí quedó dormido,
y yo le regalaba;
y el ventalle de cedros aire daba.

7. El aire de la almena,
cuando yo sus cabellos esparcía,
con su mano serena
en mi cuello hería,
y todos mis sentidos suspendía.

8. Quedéme y olvidéme,
el rostro recliné sobre el amado,
cesó todo, y dejéme,
dejando mi cuidado
entre las azucenas olvidado.

5. O dark night who guided me!
O night, kinder by far than any dawn!
O night, you who have joined
lover with beloved,
beloved into lover here transformed!

6. On my flowering bosom,
meant only for him, kept for him alone,
he rested his head to sleep,
and I with love caressed him,
and the swaying cedars sent a breeze for him.

7. The wind from the battlements
when I loosed his hair and smoothed it, unbound,
with serene and tranquil hand,
struck my neck, pierced and wounded it,
dimming and suspending all my senses.

8. I stayed there, self forgotten,
lowered my face, leaning over my lover,
all things ceased, self abandoned,
abandoning all my care
that lies, forgotten, there among the lilies.

Canción III: Llama de Amor Viva

Canciones
Del alma en la íntima comunicación
de unión de amor de Dios.

1. ¡Oh llama de amor viva
que tiernamente hieres
de mi alma en el más profundo centro!,
pues ya no eres esquiva,
acaba ya si quieres,
rompe la tela de este dulce encuentro.

2. ¡Oh cauterio suavel,
¡oh regalada llaga!
¡oh mano blanda!, ¡oh toque delicado
que a vida eterna sabe,
y toda deuda paga!
Matando, muerte en vida la has trocado.

3. ¡Oh lámparas de fuego,
en cuyos resplandores
las profundas cavernas del sentido,
que estaba oscuro y ciego,
con extraños primores
calor y luz dan junto a su querido!

4. ¡Cuán manso y amoroso
recuerdas en mi seno,
donde secretamente solo moras;
y en tu aspirar sabroso,
de bien y gloria lleno,
cuán delicadamente me enamoras!

Song III: Flame of Living Love

Songs
Of the soul in the intimate communion
of its union with God's love

1. O flame of living love
that wounds with such tenderness
the deep, the deepest center of my soul,
now that you have come to me,
conclude, if you so wish,
and rend the fabric of this sweet encounter.

2. Oh, so gentle the searing!
Oh, so delicate the wound!
Oh, sweet the hand, oh, soft so soft the blow
that tastes of life eternal
and pays each and every debt!
By killing, you have changed death into life.

3. O burning lamps of fire
in whose brilliant, searing light
the inmost caves and caverns of our senses,
which once were dark and blind,
now offer their heat and light
and give an unknown joy to their beloved!

4. How peaceful and how loving
you waken on my bosom
where you alone do dwell so secretly;
and with your perfumed breath,
so filled with good and glory,
how delicately you show your love to me.

LUIS DE GÓNGORA

(1561–1627)

Luis de Góngora was born in Córdoba, attended the University of Salamanca, and then held a benefice at the Cathedral in Córdoba. Though his life was far from austere (he was, for example, well known for his devotion to cards and bullfights, good clothes and carriages, and his association with elegant society), he was ordained as a priest in 1617. He spent the last years of his life in Madrid, where, as frequently happened in literary circles of the time, he engaged in bitter feuds with his contemporaries and arch-rivals, particularly Lope de Vega and Francisco de Quevedo.

He was a consummate master of a broad range of poetic forms, some in the popular tradition, using short pre-Renaissance lines, and others, like his sonnets, in the Italianate style introduced into Spain by Garcilaso. It was, however, the poems Góngora wrote in a *culteranista*, or euphuistic, style that earned him his reputation as a major innovator. These were his long works, *La fábula de Polifemo y Galatea* [The Fable of Polyphemus and Galatea] and *Las soledades*

[Solitudes], challenging yet exceedingly lyrical poems filled with complicated metaphors and complex imagery. At the time of their appearance (they began circulating in 1613 but were not published until after his death), they caused a great deal of controversy because of their supposedly impenetrable obscurity, and Góngora became known as the "Prince of Darkness" because he had composed them. Lope de Vega and Quevedo were enthusiastic participants in the polemics generated by Góngora's writing, and they and their followers attacked him with mocking, acerbic wit.

Unfortunately, a significant number of less-talented poets followed Góngora's stylistic lead. The anti-Góngora backlash became so strong that his poetry virtually disappeared from the poetic canon until the 1920s, when it was rediscovered and glorified by the young poets and scholars of what is called the Generation of 1927. In that year, the tricentenary of Góngora's death was celebrated in Spain by Federico García Lorca, Rafael Alberti, Dámaso Alonso, Luis Cernuda, Vicente Aleixandre, and their colleagues— an avant-garde who found in Góngora the perfect anti-romantic, anti-bourgeois voice to match their own literary commitments.

Today Góngora is recognized as a major Renaissance poet whose importance to seventeenth-century poetry is comparable to Garcilaso's influence in the sixteenth.

Soneto LXXXII

(AMOROSO)

La dulce boca que a gustar convida
un humor entre perlas destilado,
y a no invidiar aquel licor sagrado
que a Júpiter ministra el garzón de Ida,

amantes, no toquéis, si queréis vida,
porque entre un labio y otro colorado
Amor está, de su veneno armado,
cual entre flor y flor sierpe escondida.

No os engañen las rosas que, a la Aurora,
diréis que aljofaradas y olorosas
se le cayeron del purpúreo seno:

manzanas son de Tántalo, y no rosas,
que después huyen del que incitan ahora;
y sólo del amor queda el veneno.

Sonnet LXXXII
(AMOROUS)

Lovers! The sweet mouth tempting you to taste
of a liquor distilled among white pearls,
to turn from the sacred libation poured
for Jupiter by Ida's comely youth,[1]
    touch it not if you value life, for
there, between her inviting scarlet lips
is Love,[2] with deadliest poison armed,
like a serpent lurking among the blooms.
    Do not be deceived; roses that you say
have fallen, fragrant and pearly with dew,
from the purple-hued bosom of the Dawn
    are the apples of Tantalus.[3] Be warned:
they will flee the very one they tempt;
poison is all that will be left of love.

---

[1]In Greek mythology, Zeus abducted Ganymede from Mt. Ida to be his cup-bearer.

[2]Here "Love" refers to Eros or Amor, the classical god of love.

[3]In Greek mythology, the gods punished Tantalus by setting him in the middle of a lake, where he suffered intense thirst. Each time he attempted to drink, the water receded. Fruit dangled from branches above his head, but each time he tried to reach them, the branches pulled back.

Soneto CLXV

Ilustre y hermosísima María,
mientras se dejan ver a cualquier hora
en tus mejillas la rosada Aurora,
Febo en tus ojos y en tu frente el día,

y mientras con gentil descortesía
mueve el viento la hebra voladora
que la Arabia en sus venas atesora
y el rico Tajo en sus arenas cría;

antes que, de la edad Febo eclipsado
y el claro día vuelto en noche obscura,
huya la Aurora del mortal nublado;

antes que lo que hoy es rubio tesoro
venza a la blanca nieve su blancura:
goza, goza el color, la luz, el oro.

Sonnet CLXV

Luminous, most beautiful María,[1]
as long as we can see at any hour
rosy-hued Aurora[2] upon your cheek,
Phoebus[3] in your eyes, day upon your brow,
   and as long as the wind, so gently rude,
breathes upon and tousles those wafting threads
that Arabia hoards and treasures in its veins,
and wealthy Tagus gives us in its sands,[4]
   before bright Phoebus is eclipsed by time,
and clear day changes into darkest night,
making Aurora flee the mortal cloud;
   before what is today blond treasure conquers
with its own snowy whiteness the white snow:
revel, revel in color, light, and gold.

[1]The pseudonym of the girl, perhaps imagined, to whom Góngora dedicates the poem.

[2]In Roman mythology, Aurora is the goddess of the dawn.

[3]In Greek mythology, the epithet Phoebus was used to depict Apollo as god of the sun.

[4]The references are to gold: Arabia was famous for it, and the River Tagus, or Tajo, which runs through Portugal and Spain, was said to have golden sands.

Soneto CLXVI

Mientras por competir con tu cabello,
oro bruñido al sol relumbra en vano;
mientras con menosprecio en medio el llano
mira tu blanca frente el lilio bello;
    mientras a cada labio, por cogello,
siguen más ojos que al clavel temprano;
y mientras triunfa con desdén lozano
del luciente cristal tu gentil cuello:
    goza cuello, cabello, labio y frente,
antes que lo que fue en tu edad dorada
oro, lilio, clavel, cristal luciente,
    no sólo en plata o vïola troncada
se vuelva, mas tú y ello juntamente
en tierra, en humo, en polvo, en sombra, en nada.

Sonnet CLXVI

As long as burnished gold gleams in the sun
in vain, attempting to vie with your hair;
and your brow, white as snow, views with mere scorn
the lily so fair growing in the plain;
    and each lip waiting to be gathered draws
more avid eyes than first carnation blooms;
and as long as your neck so full of charm
outshines brilliant crystal with proud disdain:
    revel in neck and hair, in lip and brow
before what was in this your golden age
gold, lily, carnation, and crystal bright
    turn to silver, to violets crushed and sere,
and you and they together must become
earth, vapor, shadow, dust, nothing at all.

Romancillo XLIX

(AMOROSO)

La más bella niña
de nuestro lugar,
hoy viuda y sola,
y ayer por casar,
viendo que sus ojos
a la guerra van,
a su madre dice,
que escucha su mal:
  Dejadme llorar
  orillas del mar.

Pues me distes, madre,
en tan tierna edad
tan corto el placer,
tan largo el pesar,
y me cautivastes
de quien hoy se va
y lleva las llaves
de mi libertad:
  dejadme llorar
  orillas del mar.

En llorar conviertan
mis ojos, de hoy más,
el sabroso oficio
del dulce mirar,

Ballad XLIX

(AMOROUS)

The young girl most fair
from our little town,
now widowed, alone,
but yesterday, unwed,
sees her beloved eyes
marching off to war,
turns to her mother, who
listens as she says:
  Let me go to weep
  on the lone seashore.

Since you gave me, Mother,
at so young an age
joy that is so brief,
grief that lasts so long,
and made me captive to
the one who leaves today,
and takes with him the keys
to my own liberty:
  Let me go to weep
  on the lone seashore.

Today, oh let my eyes
turn from his sweet sight,
and now let them take up
the task of shedding tears,

pues que no se pueden
mejor ocupar,
yéndose a la guerra
quien era mi paz:
   dejadme llorar
   orillas del mar.

No me pongáis freno
ni queráis culpar;
que lo uno es justo,
lo otro por demás.
Si me queréis bien,
no me hagáis mal;
harto peor fuera
morir y callar:
   dejadme llorar
   orillas del mar.

Dulce madre mía,
¿quién no llorará,
aunque tenga el pecho
como un pedernal,
y no dará voces
viendo marchitar

for they cannot have
any better chore
when one who was my peace
marches off to war:
 Let me go to weep
 on the lone seashore.

 Do not rein me in,
or cast blame on me;
the first may well be just,
the other goes too far.
If you love me well,
do not do me harm;
it is worse for me
to die in silence drear:
 Let me go to weep
 on the lone seashore.

 Oh, sweet mother mine,
none could hold back tears
even if their hearts
were hard as flint, as stone.
Who'd not wail aloud
as the greenest years

los más verdes años
de mi mocedad?
　　Dejadme llorar
　　orillas del mar.

　　Váyanse las noches,
pues ido se han
los ojos que hacían
los míos velar;
váyanse y no vean
tanta soledad,
después que en mi lecho
sobra la mitad.
　　Dejadme llorar
　　orillas del mar.

of my fleeting youth
wither and fade away?
   Let me go to weep
   on the lone seashore.

   Let the nights leave too,
for the very eyes
that kept mine from closing
have left and gone away;
let them leave, not see
a loneliness like mine,
now that half my bed
is no use to me:
   Let me go to weep
   on the lone seashore.

Letrilla XIX

(SACRA)

Oveja perdida, ven
sobre mis hombros, que hoy
no sólo tu pastor soy,
sino tu pasto también.

Por descubrirte mejor
cuando balabas perdida,
dejé en un árbol la vida,
donde me subió el amor;
si prenda quieres mayor,
mis obras hoy te la den.
Oveja perdida, ven
sobre mis hombros, que hoy
no sólo tu pastor soy,
sino tu pasto también.

Pasto al fin hoy tuyo hecho,
¿cuál dará mayor asombro,
o el traerte yo en el hombro,
o el traerme tú en el pecho?

Lyric XIX

(SACRED)

O sheep gone astray, come
onto my shoulders, for now
I am your shepherd and more,
today I've become your food.[1]

In order to find you when
you wandered, bleating and lost,
I left my life on the tree
that my love made me ascend;[2]
if you wish a greater pledge
look to my actions today.
    O sheep gone astray, come
onto my shoulders, for now
I am your shepherd and more,
today I've become your food.

Today I become your food;
which more deeply astounds,
you on my shoulders borne, or
you holding me in your heart?

[1] The Shepherd is Jesus, the food is communion, the sheep gone astray is the soul.
[2] The tree is the cross where Christ was crucified.

Prendas son de amor estrecho
que aun los más ciegos las ven.
 Oveja perdida, ven
sobre mis hombros, que hoy
no sólo tu pastor soy,
sino tu pasto también.

These are pledges of dear love
that even the blind can see.
   O sheep gone astray, come
onto my shoulders, for now
I am your shepherd and more,
today I've become your food.

LOPE DE VEGA

(1562–1635)

Lope Félix de Vega Carpio was born into a humble family in Madrid, studied at the University of Alcalá, and led what is politely termed an "unruly" life, "combining and recombining simultaneously," as Elias Rivers has said, "his roles as lover, soldier, husband, private secretary, and priest." Lope had many love affairs and two marriages; he took part in the Invincible Armada, served as secretary to various noblemen, including the Duke of Alba, and was ordained a priest in 1614. He was a prodigiously prolific and wide-ranging writer who produced works in practically every style, from the popular to the erudite, and in every known genre, including prose fiction, narrative and lyrical poetry, and drama. He established and then dominated the popular theater in Spain, creating the tradition of the *comedia* that includes important playwrights like Pedro Calderón de la Barca, Tirso de Molina, and Juan Ruiz de Alarcón. Lope continued to be a major influence on Spanish drama throughout the seventeenth century; legend claims that, beginning at the age of thirteen, he wrote more than two thousand plays, most of them in octosyllabic and hendecasyllabic verse.

Lope composed an enormous number of poems independent of the verses he included in his prose works and his plays—an estimated three thousand sonnets in addition to verse written in other forms. For instance, his "human" poems—two hundred sonnets written in the Italianate tradition established by Garcilaso—were published as *Rimas humanas* in 1602, and his "sacred" rhymes—one hundred sonnets as well as other kinds of poems, including songs, glosses, and ballads, many of them using pre-Renaissance short-line meters—appeared *as Rimas sacras* in 1614. Two other collections of lyric poetry were published during his lifetime, and a third appeared posthumously.

Miguel de Cervantes allegedly coined the term a "monster of nature" to describe Lope because of the extent, variety, and quality of his writing. And, in fact, Lope de Vega seemed to create literature as easily as other people speak.

Rimas Sacras

I

Cuando me paro a contemplar mi estado
y a ver los pasos por donde he venido,
me espanto de que un hombre tan perdido
a conocer su error haya llegado.

Cuando miro los años que he pasado
la divina razón puesta en olvido,
conozco que piedad del cielo ha sido
no haberme en tanto mal precipitado.

Entré por laberinto tan extraño
fiando al débil hilo de la vida
el tarde conocido desengaño,

mas, de tu luz mi escuridad vencida,
el monstruo muerto de mi ciego engaño,
vuelve a la patria la razón perdida.

Sacred Rhymes

I

When I stand and contemplate my state
and look back at the path where I have trod,
I am amazed that one who went astray
so often ever came to know his fault.

When I see all the many years I spent
with back turned to the reasoned word divine,
I know that heaven's mercy, heaven's grace
saved me from falling into the devil's pit.

I walked a fearsome labyrinth in the dark,
trusting that the flimsy thread of my life
would lead me, one day, to enlightenment;[1]

but now, my ignorance conquered by your light
—the monster of blind deception slain at last—
reason can return to its rightful place.

[1] This is an allusion to the Greek myth of the Cretan Minotaur, the monster hidden away in the center of a labyrinth. A man with the head of a bull, he was defeated by Theseus, who found his way out of the labyrinth by following the thread given to him by Ariadne.

Soneto de repente

Un soneto me manda hacer Violante,
que en mi vida me he visto en tanto aprieto;
catorce versos dicen que es soneto:
burla burlando van los tres delante.

Yo pensé que no hallara consonante
y estoy a la mitad de otro cuarteto,
mas si me veo en el primer terceto,
no hay cosa en los cuartetos que me espante.

Por el primer terceto voy entrando,
y parece que entré con pie derecho,
pues fin con este verso le voy dando.

Ya estoy en el segundo, y aun sospecho
que voy los trece versos acabando;
contad si son catorce, y está hecho.

Instant Sonnet

Violante[1] orders me to write a sonnet,
I've never been so pressed in my life before.
Fourteen verses, they say, are in a sonnet:
I haven't even tried and I have four.

I thought I'd never find those fourteen lines
and here I'm halfway through another quatrain,
I only have to get to that first tercet
and then no line can ever hold me back.

And now I'm at the start of tercet one.
It seems I started out on the right foot
because with the third line here's the conclusion.

I've begun tercet two. I do believe
I'm coming to the end of thirteen verses;
see if there are fourteen: the sonnet's done.

[1]Violante is the patron, perhaps imaginary, who requests the sonnet.

Rimas Humanas
Sonnet LXI

Ir y quedarse y con quedar partirse,
partir sin alma y ir con alma ajena;
oír la dulce voz de una sirena
y no poder del árbol desasirse;

arder como la vela y consumirse
haciendo torres sobre tierna arena;
caer de un cielo y ser demonio en pena
y de serlo jamás arrepentirse;

hablar entre las mudas soledades,
pedir prestada sobre fé paciencia
y lo que es temporal llamar eterno;

creer sospechas y negar verdades
es lo que llaman en el mundo ausencia:
fuego en el alma y en la vida infierno.

Human Rhymes
Sonnet LXI

To go and stay, and staying to depart,
depart without one's soul,[1] go with another's;
to hear the siren's voice, enchanting song,
and still be bound, unwilling, to the mast,[2]

to burn like a candle, and be consumed,
to try to build a tower of soft sand;
to fall from heaven and then to become
a demon in torment, never to repent;[3]

to speak amid hushed solitudes and ask
to borrow patience, with faith as the bond,
to call eternal what is but mundane;

to trust suspicions and deny the truth,
this is what's called absence, here in the world:
a fire in the soul, and in life, hell.

[1]An allusion to the pain of leaving one's lover.

[2]In *The Odyssey*, the sirens were sea nymphs whose irresistible song lured sailors to their deaths. Odysseus ordered his crew to fill their ears with wax and then bind him to the mast so he could hear the song and survive.

[3]An allusion to the fallen angel Lucifer, thrown out of heaven and transformed into Satan when he reached earth.

Letras Varias
Canción Popular VII

No ser, Luscinda, tus bellas
niñas formalmente estrellas
bien puede ser;
pero que en su claridad
no tengan cierta deidad,
no puede ser.

Que su boca celestial
no sea el mismo coral,
bien puede ser;
mas que no exceda la rosa
en ser roja y olorosa,
no puede ser.

Que no sea el blanco pecho
de nieve o cristales hecho
bien puede ser;
mas que no exceda en blancura
cristales y nieve pura,
no puede ser.

Various Songs

FOLK SONG VII

Your beautiful eyes, Luscinda,[1]
not really stars in the sky—
that well may be;
but their brightness, their sweet light
not having something divine—
that cannot be.

Her mouth, oh heavenly sight,
not really coral itself—
that well may be;
but not surpassing the rose,
not redder, with headier scent—
that cannot be.

Her bosom, so pure and white,
not made of crystal or snow—
that well may be;
but not surpassing in whiteness
fair crystals or new-fallen snow—
that cannot be.

[1]A pseudonym for the girl, possibly imaginary, to whom the poem is
dedicated.

Que no sea sol ni Apolo,
ángel puro y fénix solo
bien puede ser;
pero que de ángel no tenga
lo que con ángel convenga,
no puede ser.

Que no sean lirios sus venas
ni sus manos azucenas,
bien puede ser,
mas que en ellas no se vean
cuantas gracias se desean,
no puede ser.

She's not the sun or Apollo,
not an angel or a phoenix[2]—
that well may be;
but that she does not possess
all that makes angels angelic—
that cannot be.

What? Not irises her veins
and not lilies those soft hands—
that well may be;
but in them not to be seen
all graces one might desire—
that cannot be.

[2]According to the Egyptian myth, as recounted by Roman writers, the phoenix, a symbol of immortality, lived for five hundred years. It killed itself by sitting in a fire, and from its ashes rose a young phoenix.

FRANCISCO DE QUEVEDO

(1580–1645)

Francisco de Quevedo was born to an aristocratic family in Madrid. He studied with the Jesuits there and then attended the University of Alcalá as well as the University of Valladolid. He was associated with the royal courts of Felipe III (1598–1621) and Felipe IV (1621–1665), making his debut at court in 1605, the year in which his first poems appeared in an anthology. Quevedo bore close witness to the political and economic decadence of Spain in the seventeenth century under the last monarchs of the House of Austrias. Serving as private secretary to the Duke of Osuna, the Spanish viceroy in Naples, Quevedo became deeply involved in the many political intrigues of the day and, when Felipe III died, suffered exile from court; by 1624 he had found favor again under Felipe IV and his minister, the Count-Duke Olivares. In 1639 he was incarcerated on mysterious charges and was not released from prison until 1643.

Quevedo was an immensely erudite, highly educated man of broad interests and profound contrasts in both his life and his writing. In the controversy generated by *culteranismo*, Góngora's euphuistic style, Quevedo was one of Góngora's most virulent enemies. He even published the works of Fray Luis de León, whom he admired greatly, in 1631, in part to provide an example of un-Gongoristic clarity in poetry. He also engaged in bitter feuds with other contemporaries, including Lope de Vega. Yet he too was associated with a manner of writing that came under critical fire, namely *conceptismo*, a style based on ingenious puns—plays of words, concepts, and conceits, comparable to what has been called "the poetry of wit and metaphysics" in England.

Quevedo was extremely prolific in a wide variety of prose and poetic genres. For instance, in 1604 he wrote one of the most mordant of the picaresque novels, *El Buscón* [The Swindler], which had countless revisions imposed on it because of religious censorship; consequently, it was not published until 1626. The highly imaginative and bitterly satiric *Sueños* [Dreams] appeared in 1627. Yet Quevedo was also capable of the most exalted lyricism and profound meditation. He wrote more than nine hundred poems—amorous, philosophical, satirical, patriotic, or pious—in a broad range of forms and meters. These works were grouped according to theme only after his death.

At his best, Quevedo achieved a deeply lyrical, highly intelligent voice. If he had written nothing but his incomparably profound, contemplative sonnets, he would still be considered a major European poet.

Poemas Metafísicos

2

Represéntase la brevedad de lo que se vive
y cuán nada parece lo que se vivió

«¡Ah de la vida!» . . . ¿Nadie me responde?
¡Aquí de los antaños que he vivido!
La Fortuna mis tiempos ha mordido;
las Horas mi locura las esconde.

    ¡Que sin poder saber cómo ni adónde,
la salud y la edad se hayan huído!
Falta la vida, asiste lo vivido,
y no hay calamidad que no me ronde.

    Ayer se fue; mañana no ha llegado;
hoy se está yendo sin parar un punto;
soy un fue, y un será, y un es cansado.

    En el hoy y mañana y ayer, junto
pañales y mortaja, y he quedado
presentes sucesiones de difunto.

Metaphysical Poems

2

*Which represents the brevity of our present life
and the apparent nothingness of our past life*

"Hear me, ah my life!" What? Does none respond?
Bring back those days I lived so long ago.
Fortune has gnawed at my allotted time,
and my own folly hides the passing hours.

Ah, not knowing how or where they have gone,
my health and youth and time are lost to me!
I have no life except what I have lived,
nothing but misfortune hovers round.

Yesterday's gone, tomorrow's not yet come,
Today's in headlong flight and will not stop;
I am a weary was, will be, and is.

In my today, tomorrow, yesterday
I join swaddling and shroud, and have become
present successions of the same dead man.

Poemas Metafísicos

3

Significase la propria brevedad de la vida,
sin pensar y con padecer,
salteada de la muerte

¡Fue sueño ayer; mañana será tierra!
¡Poco antes, nada; y poco después, humo!
¡Y destino ambiciones, y presumo
apenas punto al cerco que me cierra!

Breve combate de importuna guerra,
en mi defensa soy peligro sumo;
y mientras con mis armas me consumo,
menos me hospeda el cuerpo, que me entierra.

Ya no es ayer; mañana no ha llegado;
hoy pasa, y es, y fue, con movimiento
que a la muerte me lleva despeñado.

Azadas son la hora y el momento,
que, a jornal de mi pena y mi cuidado,
cavan en mi vivir mi monumento.

Metaphysical Poems

3

*Which indicates the brevity of life,
unthinking and suffering,
under assault by death*

Yesterday a dream and tomorrow dust!
Not long ago, nothing, and soon mere smoke!
And I pursue ambitions, and presume,
though just a point in this encircling siege!
   Brief combat in a bloody, hard-fought war,
I am the greatest threat to my defense;
as my own weapons do me gravest harm
this body is less host and more my tomb.
   Yesterday's over, tomorrow's not yet come,
today passes, is, was, and as it moves
it sweeps me down into the abyss of death.
   The hour and the minute are the spades
that, paid for by my sorrow and my grief,
dig my grave in the soil of my own life.

Poemas Metafísicos

6

Arrepentimiento y lágrimas
debidas al engaño de la vida

Huye sin percibirse, lento, el día,
y la hora secreta y recatada
con silencio se acerca, y, despreciada,
lleva tras sí la edad lozana mía.

La vida nueva, que en niñez ardía,
la juventud robusta y engañada,
en el postrer invierno sepultada,
yace entre negra sombra y nieve fría.

No sentí resbalar mudos los años;
hoy los lloro pasados, y los veo
riendo de mis lágrimas y daños.

Mi penitencia deba a mi deseo,
pues me deben la vida mis engaños,
y espero el mal que paso, y no le creo.

6

*Repentance and tears
    caused by the deception of life*

The day slips away, undetected, slow;
in secrecy and stealth a silent hour
comes near, scorned and maligned, to take from me
the gallantry and charm of treasured youth.
    New life flamed so bright when I was a boy,
my youthful days, robust and yet deceived
are buried in the final wintry cold,
lying between black shade and freezing snow.
    I did not hear the mute years steal away;
today I weep their passing and can see
them laughing at my tears and all my care.
    Let penance owe a debt to my desire
for my illusions all owe their life to me.
I wait for present grief I do not think will come.

Poemas Metafísicos

8

Conoce la diligencia con que se acerca
la muerte, y procura conocer también
la conveniencia de su venida,
y aprovecharse de ese conocimiento

Ya formidable y espantoso suena
dentro del corazón el postrer día;
y la última hora, negra y fría,
se acerca, de temor y sombras llena.
    Si agradable descanso, paz serena
la muerte en traje de dolor envía,
señas da su desdén de cortesía:
más tiene de caricia que de pena.
    ¿Qué pretende el temor desacordado
de la que a rescatar piadosa viene
espíritu en miseries anudado?
    Llegue rogada, pues mi bien previene;
hálleme agradecido, no asustado;
mi vida acabe, y mi vivir ordene.

8

Which acknowledges the speed with which Death
approaches, and attempts to acknowledge as well
the correctness of her arrival,
and to make good use of it.

Formidable and fearsome now resounds
within my heart the ultimate last day;
and the final hour, so black, so cold,
approaches, full of terror, full of dark.

If sweet tranquility and peace serene
Death, in the garb of grief, does send to us,
then her harsh rigor's a sign of courtesy:
less punishment and more a fond caress.

To what end do we feel discordant terror
of one, compassionate, who comes to save
a spirit trapped in snares of misery?

Let her be welcome: she prepares my good;
let her find me grateful, not filled with fear;
let her end my life and ordain my living.[1]

[1]The essential trope is the religious belief that physical death allows for the eternal life of the soul.

Poemas Amorosos

471

Cerrar podrá mis ojos la postrera
sombra que me llevare el blanco día,
y podrá desatar esta alma mía
hora a su afán ansioso lisonjera;
  mas no, de esotra parte, en la ribera,
dejará la memoria, en donde ardía:
nadar sabe mi llama la agua fría,
y perder el respeto a ley severa.
  Alma a quien todo un dios prisión ha sido,
venas que humor a tanto fuego han dado,
medulas que han gloriosamente ardido:
  su cuerpo dejará, no su cuidado;
serán ceniza, mas tendrá sentido;
polvo serán, mas polvo enamorado.

Amorous Poems

471

Love that is constant after death

The final dark may close these eyes of mine
and take from me the pure white light of day,
a generous final hour may set free
my soul, longing to realize its desire,

   but on that other shore it will not leave
or lose the memory in which it burned:[1]
this flame of mine can swim the icy flow
and set aside the rigors of harsh law.

   My soul imprisoned by a mighty god,[2]
these veins whose humor[3] fueled the raging fire,
this marrow that so gloriously burned

   may leave behind this flesh but not love's pangs;
they will be ash but ash that still can feel,
they will be dust but dust that is in love.

---

[1]In classical mythology, the River Styx surrounded Hades, where Charon ferried the souls of the dead, who were supposed to lose their memory of life on earth.

[2]The god of love in classical mythology.

[3]The reference is to the ancient medical theory of the four humors (blood, phlegm, black bile, and yellow bile). The humor in the veins is blood, associated with a fiery, passionate temperament.

Salmo XVII

Miré los muros de la patria mía,
si un tiempo fuertes, ya desmoronados,
de la carrera de la edad cansados,
por quien caduca ya su valencía.
    Salíme al campo; vi que el sol bebía
los arroyos del yelo desatados,
y del monte quejosos los ganados,
que con sombras hurtó su luz al día.
    Entré en mi casa; vi que, amancillada,
de anciana habitación era despojos;
mi báculo, más corvo y menos fuerte.
    Vencida de la edad sentí mi espada,
y no hallé cosa en que poner los ojos
que no fuese recuerdo de la muerte.

Psalm XVII

    I looked upon the walls of my native land,
at one time strong, now crumbling and decayed,
wearied by the unceasing race of time
that weakens virtue and makes valor fail.
    I went out to the fields and saw the sun
drinking up streams that had been freed from ice,
and cattle that lamented gloomy peaks
using their shadows to rob day of its light.
    I entered my house, saw how it was stained,
the wreckage of an ancient dwelling place,
my staff more bent, and of its strength bereft,
    my sword, I felt, now overcome by age;
no matter where I turned my eyes I found
nothing that did not make me think of death.

Salmo XVIII

Todo tras sí lo lleva el año breve
de la vida mortal, burlando el brío
al acero valiente, al mármol frío,
que contra el Tiempo su dureza atreve.

Antes que sepa andar el pie, se mueve
camino de la muerte, donde envío
mi vida oscura: pobre y turbio río
que negro mar con altas ondas bebe.

Todo corto momento es paso largo
que doy, a mi pesar, en tal jornada,
pues, parado y durmiendo, siempre aguijo.

Breve suspiro, y último, y amargo,
es la muerte, forzosa y heredada:
mas si es ley, y no pena, ¿qué me aflijo?

Psalm XVIII

The too-brief year of this our mortal life
sweeps everything away, mocking the courage
of valiant steel and marble gleaming cold
that dare to challenge time with their hard strength.
    Before my foot knows how to walk it moves
along the path to death, where I do send
my obscure life, a poor and turbulent river
swallowed by great waves in a pitch-black sea.
    Each brief moment a long and thrusting step
I take against my will, for on this journey
e'en when still, or sleeping, I spur ahead.
    A brief lament, a final, bitter sigh
is death, the fate that is our legacy:
if law, not penalty, why do I grieve?

Salmo XIX

¡Cómo de entre mis manos te resbalas!
¡Oh, cómo te deslizas, edad mía!
¡Qué mudos pasos traes, oh muerte fría,
pues con callado pie todo lo igualas!
    Feroz, de tierra el débil muro escalas,
en quien lozana juventud se fía;
mas ya mi corazón del postrer día
atiende el vuelo, sin mirar las alas.
    ¡Oh condición mortal! ¡Oh dura suerte!
¡Que no puedo querer vivir mañana
sin la pensión de procurar mi muerte!
    Cualquier instante de la vida humana
es nueva ejecución, con que me advierte
cuán frágil es, cuán mísera, cuán vana . . .

Psalm XIX

Oh, how you slip away between my hands!
My allotted time, how you slide away!
Oh, icy Death, what muted steps you take,
those silent feet leveling all there is!
Fiercely you scale a weakened wall of earth,[1]
the one upon which gallant youth depends,
but my heart now awaits the deadly flight
of the final day, not looking at the wings.
Oh, mortal fate! Oh, pitiless destiny!
I cannot wish to still live on the morrow
and not pay the cost by seeking my own death!
Any instant of this, our human life,
is one more execution, warning me
how fragile and wretched it is, all vanity . . .

[1]In the context of the poem's martial imagery, the "wall of earth" alludes to
the human body.

SOR JUANA INÉS DE LA CRUZ
(1651?–1695)

B orn Juana de Asbaje y Ramírez, in San Miguel Nepantla, near Mexico City, Sor Juana, as she is known today, was the presumably illegitimate daughter of a middle-class Mexican mother and a Spanish Basque father, a man about whom almost nothing else is known. Juana de Asbaje was intellectually precocious and was taken to the viceregal court in the capital while still very young. She learned Latin quickly, and became well known for her erudition as well as for her exceptional beauty. She served for some years as a lady-in-waiting to the vice-reine Mancera.

Asbaje entered the Convent of San Jerónimo (*Sor* is her religious title) in 1669, apparently to avoid marriage and continue her studies, a course of action taken by many intellectual women in Europe and the Americas during this period in order to escape the limitations in the secular world on their ability to study and write. She composed a good amount of poetry for religious celebrations, as well as works in the amorous tradition; her poems first appeared in

Madrid in 1689. She wrote plays based on both secular and religious themes, and a long work, *Primero sueño* [First Dream], is considered the most accomplished philosophical poem of the Golden Age. In this, and in other pieces, including sixty-three sonnets in the high Renaissance style, Sor Juana is the intellectual and lyrical heir to the *conceptismo* of Quevedo and the *culteranismo* of Góngora; she is still referred to today as "The Tenth Muse."

In 1690 she became embroiled in controversy when, at the request of Manuel Fernández de Santa Cruz, the Bishop of Puebla, she criticized Antonio Vieyra, a Jesuit preacher, on the basis of patristic theological concepts. She received a mild reprimand from the bishop, who wrote to her under the pseudonym of "Sor Filotea," and in her eloquent response of 1691, *Respuesta a Sor Filotea de la Cruz* [An Answer to Sor Filotea de la Cruz], she defended her commitment to a life of the intellect. But then, perhaps as a consequence of the enemies she had made within the Church because of her intellectual acuity and independence, this immensely gifted poet stopped studying, sold her library of more than four thousand volumes—the largest in Mexico at the time—and donated the proceeds to charitable causes. She died a few years later while caring for other nuns during an epidemic.

Soneto 145

Procura desmentir los elogios que a un retrato
de la Poetisa inscribió la verdad,
que llama pasión.

Este, que ves, engaño colorido,
que del arte ostentando los primores,
con falsos silogismos de colores
es cauteloso engaño del sentido;

    éste, en quien la lisonja ha pretendido
excusar de los años los horrores,
y venciendo del tiempo los rigores,
triunfar de la vejez y del olvido,

    es un vano artificio del cuidado,
es una flor al viento delicada,
es un resguardo inútil para el hado;

    es una necia diligencia errada,
es un afán caduco y, bien mirado,
es cadáver, es polvo, es sombra, es nada.

Sonnet 145

In which she attempts to refute the praises
of a portrait of the poet, signed by truth,
which she calls passion

This thing you see, a bright-colored deceit,
displaying all the many charms of art,
with false syllogisms of tint and hue
is a cunning deception of the eye;
    this thing in which sheer flattery has tried
to evade the stark horrors of the years
and, vanquishing the cruelties of time,
to triumph over age and oblivion,
    is vanity, contrivance, artifice,
a delicate blossom stranded in the wind,
a failed defense against our common fate;
    a fruitless enterprise, a great mistake,
a decrepit frenzy, and rightly viewed,
a corpse, some dust, a shadow, mere nothingness.

Soneto 147

En que da moral censura a una rosa,
y en ella a sus semejantes.

Rosa divina que en gentil cultura
eres, con tu fragrante sutileza,
magisterio purpúreo en la belleza,
enseñanza nevada a la hermosura;

   amago de la humana arquitectura,
ejemplo de la vana gentileza,
en cuyo sér unió naturaleza
la cuna alegre y triste sepultura:

   ¡cuán altiva en tu pompa, presumida,
soberbia, el riesgo de morir desdeñas,
y luego desmayada y encogida

   de tu caduco sér das mustias señas,
con que con docta muerte y necia vida,
viviendo engañas y muriendo enseñas!

Sonnet 147

*In which she morally censures a rose,
and thereby all that resemble it*

O rose divine, in gentle cultivation
you are, with all your fragrant subtlety,
tuition, purple-hued, to loveliness,
snow-white instruction to the beautiful;
    intimation of a human structure,
example of gentility in vain,
in whose one being nature has united
the joyful cradle and the mournful grave;
    how haughty in your pomp, presumptuous one,
how proud when you disdain the threat of death,
then, in a swoon and shriveling, you give
    a withered vision of a failing self;
and so, with your wise death and foolish life,
in living you deceive, dying you teach!

Soneto 148

Escoge antes el morir que exponerse
a los ultrajes de la vejez.

Miró Celia una rosa que en el prado
ostentaba feliz la pompa vana
y con afeites de carmín y grana
bañaba alegre el rostro delicado;

    y dijo:—Goza, sin temor del Hado,
el curso breve de tu edad lozana,
pues no podrá la muerte de mañana
quitarte lo que hubieres hoy gozado;

    y aunque llega la muerte presurosa
y tu fragante vida se te aleja,
no sientas el morir tan bella y moza:

    mira que la experiencia te aconseja
que es fortuna morirte siendo hermosa
y no ver el ultraje de ser vieja.

Sonnet 148

She prefers to die rather than expose herself
to the indignities of old age.

Celia[1] looked at a rose that in the meadow
so happily displayed vain pomp and show,
and with creams of scarlet and crimson paint
gaily drenched and daubed her lovely face;
    and Celia said: "Enjoy with no fear of fate
the too-brief course of this your flowering youth,
for never can the death that comes tomorrow
take away from you the joy of today;
    and even though death hurries and hastens near
and fragrant life leaves and abandons you,
do not lament your dying fair and young:
    remember—the wisdom of the world will say
you were fortunate to die while beautiful
and not endure the indignity of age."

[1]Celia is a frequent name in the pastoral tradition.

Soneto 164

En que satisface un recelo con la retórica del llanto.

Esta tarde, mi bien, cuando te hablaba,
como en tu rostro y tus acciones vía
que con palabras no te persuadía,
que el corazón me vieses deseaba;

　y Amor, que mis intentos ayudaba,
venció lo que imposible parecía:
pues entre el llanto, que el dolor vertía,
el corazón deshecho destilaba.

　Baste ya de rigores, mi bien, baste;
no te atormenten más celos tiranos,
ni el vil recelo tu quietud contraste

　con sombras necias, con indicios vanos,
pues ya en líquido humor viste y tocaste
mi corazón deshecho entre tus manos.

Sonnet 164

In which she responds to jealous suspicion with the rhetoric of weeping

This afternoon, my love, when I spoke to you,
I could see in your face, in what you did,
that you were not persuaded by mere words,
and I wished you could see into my heart;

and Love,[1] assisting me in my attempt,
overcame the seeming impossible,
for among the tears that my sorrow shed
was my breaking heart, liquid and distilled.

Enough of anger now, my love, enough;
do not let tyrant jealousy torment you,
nor base suspicion roil your serenity

with foolish specters and deceptive clues;
in liquid humor[2] you have seen and touched
my broken heart and held it in your hands.

[1]The reference is to the classical god of love.
[2]Humor here refers to a bodily fluid.

Soneto 165

Que contiene una fantasía contenta con amor decente.

Détente, sombra de mi bien esquivo,
imagen del hechizo que más quiero,
bella ilusión por quien alegre muero,
dulce ficción por quien penosa vivo.

Si al imán de tus gracias, atractivo,
sirve mi pecho de obediente acero,
¿para qué me enamoras lisonjero
si has de burlarme luego fugitivo?

Mas blasonar no puedes, satisfecho,
de que triunfa de mí tu tiranía:
que aunque dejas burlado el lazo estrecho

que tu forma fantástica ceñía,
poco importa burlar brazos y pecho
si te labra prisión mi fantasía.

Sonnet 165

Which restrains a fantasy by making it content with decent love

Halt, O faint shade of my elusive love,
image of the enchantment I love best,
fair illusion for whom I gladly die,
sweet fiction for whose sake I live in pain.

   If th'attraction, the magnet of your charms
draws my heart as if it were made of steel,
why woo and win me over with flattery
if then you will deceive me, turn and flee?

   But, satisfied and proud, you cannot boast
that your tyranny triumphs over me:
for though you escape and slip through the tight ropes

   that bind your imagined form in fantasy,
it matters not if you elude my arms,
my heart, when my thought alone can imprison you.